What beyond ordinary leaders are saying about Scott George and *Living Beyond Ordinary: Discovering Authentic Significance and Purpose:*

"Living Beyond Ordinary is the inspirational account of how an ordinary life, fueled by an extraordinary vision, can help to change a community one life at a time."

Congressman Daniel Webster

"I am excited Scott George has shared his experiences in his new book, **Living Beyond Ordinary: Discovering Authentic Significance and Purpose.** *The story of how Scott started this charity outreach—with one pallet of food and sheer dedication and determination— is truly an inspiration. Scott's vision has motivated many people in our community to help thousands of families obtain a better quality of life. I admire and appreciate his vision and insight."*

Mayor Buddy Dyer
City of Orlando

"Orange County, Florida is fortunate to have Scott George and his leadership. The Community Food and Outreach Center makes our community a better place to live."

Teresa Jacobs
Orange County Mayor

"Pastor Scott George is somewhat of a hero in our community—a man who acted out of faith and loved out of compassion. This book will not only inspire you, it will make you want to help someone . . . or even accomplish your own God-given dreams."

Dr. Joel C. Hunter, Senior Pastor
Northland, A Church Distributed

"What a gripping story of a modern-day Nehemiah dramatically called to rebuild the broken people of Orlando, my hometown. The innovative ideas in this book are every bit as original as the iPhone or Google. Scott George and his team are doing for food what Habitat for Humanity did for homes—giving people the human dignity of participating in their own rescue and recovery. If you want to be inspired to do something beyond ordinary, this is the book for you; but block out some time, because once you start, it'll be hard to put down!"

Pat Morley
Author, Founder of Man in the Mirror

"Living Beyond Ordinary is an eloquent, thoughtful, and inspirational story, shared by of one of Central Florida's truly selfless servants. The Orlando Solar Bear organization is proud to call Scott George a friend and colleague."

Jason Siegel, CEO/President
Orlando Solar Bears

"Living Beyond Ordinary reflects what is possible when a man of God commits to do the unglamorous ministry of providing for those truly in need."

Dick Batchelor, Founder and President
Dick Batchelor Management Group, Inc.

"Scott George's book, Living Beyond Ordinary, takes us on a journey, revealing a fresh, life-changing look at how we can carry out the mission of Christ's compassion."

Dr. David Uth, Senior Pastor
First Baptist Orlando

"As you read this book, it will inspire you to fight the enemy called average and motivate you to passionately pursue a life beyond ordinary."

Andrae Bailey, CEO
Central Florida Commission on Homelessness

----

*"Scott George and the mission of the Community Food and Outreach Center have impacted thousands of lives in Central Florida. The hopeless now have hope, thanks to this man's philosophy of giving a hand up instead of a hand out, and the message of **Living Beyond Ordinary.**"*

Scott Anez, Broadcaster
ESPN Radio
WDBO, Orlando FL

----

*"Scott George and this book, **Living Beyond Ordinary**, are true blessings to our community and to those well beyond Central Florida who will be impacted by this positive, life-changing message. He exemplifies living a life beyond the ordinary.*

Jason Brewer, Meteorologist
WESH-TV, Orlando FL

----

*"Scott George has long been a selfless, faithful leader in our community. I know this book, **Living Beyond Ordinary**, will be an inspiration to many."*

Dr. David Swanson, Senior Pastor
First Presbyterian Church of Orlando

"Scott's vision to build the Community Food and Outreach Center, a place of hope that provides a helping hand to others, is a testament to his core beliefs."

Pete Clarke
Orange County Commissioner

----

*"In **Living Beyond Ordinary**, Pastor Scott George has actually written three books in one—an exciting and inspirational story, a carefully considered philosophy of what true charity entails, and a powerful message about God's call to each of us to make a decided difference in a world of great need."*

James Coffin, Executive Director
Interfaith Council of Central Florida

"Scott George is a genuine, straightforward follower of Jesus, with a big heart and a sharp mind who has developed an amazing, innovative, and pace-setting ministry in Central Florida. Scott's leadership gifts and passion for others clearly are beyond ordinary."

Dr. Bob Bushong
Senior Pastor/Minister of Preaching
First United Methodist Church

----

*"As a guest lecturer at the University of Central Florida's MBA Executive Leadership courses, Scott George shared his huge heart and great wisdom, just as he does in **Living Beyond Ordinary**. This book will powerfully challenge you to make a positive difference in each life you touch."*

Greg Mathison Sr., M.S., Ph.D.
University of Central Florida

----

*"**Living Beyond Ordinary** is a compelling and inspiring story that challenges all of us to fight average and live our lives with a sense of urgency and purpose."*

Austin Hunt, CEO and Founder
Harvest Food Outreach

Living Beyond Ordinary

Discovering Authentic Significance and Purpose

Scott George

Living Beyond Ordinary
Scott George

By George Publishing
Orlando, Florida

Library of Congress Control Number: 2014942621

ISBN: 978-1-940243-39-9

Some names and identifying details have been changed to protect the privacy of individuals.

All Scripture quotations designated (NIV) are taken from the Holy Bible, New International Version® NIV® Copyright © 1973, 1978, 1984, 2011 by Biblica, Inc.® Used by permission. All rights reserved worldwide.

Scripture designated (MSG) taken from The Message. Copyright © 1993, 1994, 1995, 1996, 2000, 2001, 2002. Used by permission of NavPress Publishing Group.

Scripture designated (NASB) taken from the NEW AMERICAN STANDARD BIBLE®, Copyright © 1960, 1962, 1963, 1968, 1971, 1972, 1973, 1975, 1977, 1995 by The Lockman Foundation. Used by permission.

Scripture designated (NKJV) taken from the New King James Version®. Copyright © 1982 by Thomas Nelson, Inc. Used by permission. All rights reserved.

Scripture designated (ASV) is in the public domain.

DEDICATION

My hope is for
The underdog
The dark horse
The long shot
And the sleeper to discover purpose and significance in these
pages.

My wish is that the words in this book will inspire
The haves
The have-nots
The down-and-outers
And the up-and-comers to dream again and live outside the box.

My prayer is that those who have been labeled
Unlikely
Unlovely
Unlucky
And unlovable will find a sense of destiny and grace to move
forward.

ACKNOWLEDGMENTS

~ To my Savior & Lord . . . Thank you for using me to expand your kingdom, not mine.

~ To my wife, Tammi . . . You've been my best friend for over thirty-five years; here's to another thirty-five!

~ To my children, Austen, Aaren, Amanda, and Allison . . . You make me proud. Being your dad is one of my greatest joys.

~ To my parents, Jim and Bobbie George . . . Your faith and godly example have been a strong foundation for me.

~ To my brother, Kris . . . You're the greatest brother I could ask for.

~ To my Pine Castle United Methodist Church family . . . I love leading you and worshipping with you each Sunday.

~ To my Community Food and Outreach Center (CFOC) staff and board . . . Thank you for sharing your passion with me to offer hope to families in need.

~ To Dee Lindley . . . Your endless help has inspired me to do more. I'm so glad you're "here to help."

~ To Dave Siriano at Shiny Head Productions . . . Your video expertise and passion for helping others is contagious.

~ To Jim Kochenburger . . . Your wisdom and insight on this project have been spot on.

"Watch your thoughts, they become words.

Watch your words, they become actions.

Watch your actions, they become habits.

Watch your habits, they become your character.

Watch your character, it becomes your destiny."

—Frank Outlaw

TABLE OF CONTENTS

INTRODUCTION

"An original is hard to find but easy to recognize." —John Mason

"Success is doing ordinary things extraordinarily well."—Jim Rohn

"A hero is no braver than an ordinary man, but he is brave five minutes longer."—Ralph Waldo Emerson

"I don't work at being ordinary."—Paul McCartney

"Be daring, be different, be impractical, be anything that will assert integrity of purpose and imaginative vision against the play-it-safers, the creatures of the commonplace, the slaves of the ordinary."—Cecil Beaton

"I think a hero is an ordinary individual who finds strength to persevere and endure in spite of overwhelming obstacles." —Christopher Reeve

"You were born an original, don't die a copy." —John Mason

"If you are not willing to risk the unusual, you will have to settle for the ordinary."—Jim Rohn

Or•di•nar•y [awr-dn-er-ee]

1. of no special quality or interest; commonplace; unexceptional
2. plain or undistinguished
3. somewhat inferior or below average; mediocre
4. customary; usual; normal; the commonplace or average condition, degree; something regular, usual

What is a life beyond ordinary?

Something just didn't sound right about the words I read as I looked up the word "ordinary": "plain, average, normal, commonplace." Ordinary certainly wasn't appealing to me, nor did it make me want to wake up in the morning with the goal of being plain. I tend to agree with Lou Holtz, the great football coach and sports personality, when he said, "I can't believe that God put us on this earth to be ordinary."

Don't get me wrong, I'm a pretty ordinary guy. I'm a pastor and nonprofit founder in Orlando. I've been married to my best friend, Tammi, for twenty-nine years, and we have four great children. There is nothing really very special about me other than the fact that I've seen some remarkable events take place in my life over the last few years in starting the nonprofit Community Food and Outreach Center in downtown Orlando.

From our beginning thirteen years ago, I have chronicled amazing stories and experiences I believe will inspire and motivate ordinary people to become extraordinary. Plus, over the past thirty years of leading organizations, churches, nonprofit centers and people, I have learned a few things about people and their dreams that I know will help you live a beyond ordinary life.

What do you want to be when you grow up?

In 1968, the Detroit Tigers played the St. Louis Cardinals in the World Series. Our family had just moved from Detroit to Missouri, and everyone in my class at school was consumed with the baseball battle. I soon figured out that I was the only one in that class of thirty-five kids who was rooting for the underdog Tigers. My classmates couldn't believe I could actually live in Missouri and root for a team in Michigan. They didn't understand it and neither did I. All I knew was that I was determined that no matter the cost, I would remain a loyal fan until the bitter end. Although I was only seven years old, I learned a very important lesson that fall that would follow me the rest of my life: Cheering for the underdog can be a bit intimidating and lonely, but very rewarding.

I had no idea that this characteristic would follow me and shape my calling and ministry. However, ever since that series I always find myself rooting for the team no one seems to want to win. I loved the fact that the very team the experts said could not win, actually did win, pulling off the upset. So even as a young boy, I found great reward in believing for the one no one wanted to win. Whether a baseball team or the kid sitting alone in the lunchroom, I found myself being drawn to the unpopular and rejected—those others had written off.

As children, we all have superheroes we look up to and admire, and sometimes try to imitate. We love the fact that Superman shows up at just the right time and saves the day, or how Batman knows exactly what to do to rescue a person in need. As a kid, I never really had a specific superhero I wanted to be when I grew up, but I do remember the joy I felt when I stood up for the kid being made fun of, befriended the new kid on the block who needed a friend, or encouraged a friend who needed to be cheered up. I wasn't much for following the crowd. Even as a young boy, I was willing to go against the flow and cheer loudly for the underdog. Although the Tigers eventually won the series that year, I was the real winner by learning the principle of being a hero for those in need.

Most people grow up believing that one day they will be great and do great things. Ask any little kid what they want to do when they grow up and I guarantee they won't say, "I want to be normal" or "I want to be average." No, most little children have within them a seed of greatness to be extraordinary.

However, for many of us, over time, our dreams get dashed. We slip into a commonplace life and forget about the dreams and goals we once had. I tend to agree with Ralph Waldo Emerson, who said, "Most men lead lives of quiet desperation and go to the grave with the song still in them." Most people live their lives with a song in their heart, but they have lost the tune or forgotten the words, and they are living commonplace, normal lives.

"Most people live their lives with a song in their heart, but they have lost the tune or forgotten the words, and they are living commonplace, normal lives."

There are currently eight billion people alive in this world, and the number is growing. I want you to be inspired to believe that you were born to live beyond ordinary. You may be one of eight billion, but you were not created to simply lead a life of quiet desperation. You were created to lead a life of extraordinary greatness.

In this book, I will share stories and experiences from my own life and work that will contain principles you can apply to your own life to move beyond ordinary to find significance and purpose. I hope this will inspire you to reach back to your childhood dreams of being great and achieving greatness. Since I'm not only an author, speaker, and nonprofit leader, but a pastor as well, I will add to the recipe the spice that makes greatness and beyond ordinary living possible . . . the God factor. I believe you will see the value of time-tested biblical principles that apply to any situation or circumstance. I really believe what Mike Huckabee says: "It's when ordinary people rise above the expectations and seize the opportunity that milestones truly are reached." God has a way of using ordinary people to do extraordinary things.

Let's get started on our journey together to living the beyond ordinary life.

Stay Connected!

At the end of each chapter, I include a video featuring valuable insights into living a beyond ordinary life. Be sure to download a barcode/QR code scanner app to your smartphone or tablet to view these videos. I also provide the video links so you have the option to enter them into your web browser to view the videos.

Social Media

Connect with us through social media. Encourage others to do so as well, so they can learn the principles and practices of those who live beyond ordinary lives.

 Follow me on Twitter: @RevJScottGeorge (https://twitter.com/RevJScottGeorge/)

 Become a fan on Facebook: J scott george (https://www.facebook.com/pages/J-scott-george/668980636 525535)

 Connect with me on LinkedIn: J Scott George (https://www.linkedin.com/profile/view?id=237735739)
Watch our videos: http://www.jscottgeorge.com/

Websites

www.livingbeyondordinary.org

www.communityfoodoutreach.org

Email

Jscottgeorge1@gmail.com

Scott George

"If you change the way you look at things, the things you look at change."—Wayne Dyer

~

"It's not what you look at that matters, it's what you see."
—Henry David Thoreau

~

"Open your eyes, look within. Are you satisfied with the life you're living?" —Bob Marley

~

"Life's most persistent question is, 'What are you doing for others?'"—Dr. Martin Luther King

~

"I was not a messiah, but an ordinary man who had become a leader because of extraordinary circumstances."—Nelson Mandela

~

CHAPTER 1

BEYOND ORDINARY LIVING

The Miller family met me in my church office in the darkest moment of their life. Mr. Miller was a Vietnam veteran who had defended our country with honor and courage; yet now, the Miller's house was a few weeks away from foreclosure, their eight-year-old daughter, Amanda, was facing a serious illness and needed immediate medical treatment. Unpaid bills were piling up, and they were hungry. In complete desperation, they looked to God, His church—His people—for help. My heart was broken for them, but I also knew the sad truth: We were unable to meet their needs. Guilt and shame washed over me.

I was fully aware of what the Bible says about not sending away people in need, but I had a budget to adhere to and a bottom line to keep an eye on. Despite my feelings of guilt, I had to deliver the devastating news: "I'm sorry . . . we can't help you." Even as the words came out of my mouth, my shame increased and grew. They seemed a bit confused at my answer, inadvertently glancing around at the nicely furnished church office as if to ask, "How is that possible? Look at this place!" No doubt, they had seen the fairly new cars of our staff members as they walked through our parking lot, and as they entered the building, noticed the fine new sound system and beautiful organ in the sanctuary. They could only imagine what the office furniture alone cost. They were right to be perplexed.

I offered to pray for them, hoping this would relieve my embarrassment, but it didn't. The more I prayed for them, the worse I felt. After my faithless prayer, my goal was to escort them out of my office as quickly as possible, hoping that as soon as they were gone, my shame would be gone as well; however, after they left it only weighed heavy on my heart.

I watched the Millers leave my office and walk south on Orange Avenue in downtown Orlando. They left facing homelessness, unable to care for their young daughter's serious medical condition, and uncertain what they would even eat that day.

Soon after, I left my plush office, got into my new Chevy Suburban, and drove north on Orange Avenue, toward the suburbs. I hoped my thirty-minute commute would be filled with smooth jazz to help me relax and find some rationalization to relieve my guilt and shame over my encounter just minutes earlier with the Millers. Yet with every mile I drove, the conviction that something was very wrong only increased. I compared the Miller's current life situation with my own. I had a roof over my head. They would soon be homeless. Dinner was waiting for me. They didn't know where their next meal would come from. Should any medical issue arise for my children, I had the medical coverage and money to cover it. Their daughter might die without treatment. My thirty-minute commute felt like three hours—the longest ride of my life.

I tried to encourage myself with reminders that I was a loving man and that ours was a giving, generous church, and recalled many examples to make a convincing case for this. It didn't help. *Though we could not help the Millers today, many families are in need, and we have helped many*, I reassured myself. It didn't work. I tried to comfort myself with the thought that our church was certainly not as bad as some at helping those in need. No relief. I tried to console myself with the thought that we were doing as much as the *average, ordinary* Christian church. This hit me like a freight train: a*verage . . . ordinary.*

There it was. In that instant, God seared my heart with the truth that He was calling our church—and me personally—to live beyond ordinary.

"In that instant, God seared my heart with the truth that He was calling our church—and me personally— to live beyond ordinary."

This was a turning point in my life and in my faith. God broke my heart and I could only cry out to Him for mercy and forgiveness. For the rest of that ride, I prayed fervently, committing our church and myself to never repeat what I had done that day. Never again would we turn our ear from the cries of the poor. Never again would we settle for living an ordinary Christian life. From that time on, we were determined to *live beyond ordinary* (#LivingBeyondOrdinary).

It All Started with a Pallet of Food

Our church in Winter Park, Florida (just north of the Orlando city limits), was started by a small, motley crew of passionate college students with big hearts and big vision. We were determined that our DNA would be different from the churches we had known, yet we had not fully realized our vision. Though many consider Winter Park to be an affluent area, energized by our resolve to move beyond ordinary, we were determined to commit significant time and energy to reaching our community by helping people in practical ways.

We picked up a single $65 pallet of food from the local food bank and began distributing it to those in need. It wasn't much, but it was all we could afford, and an important first step of obedience.

Though we were not sure if what we were doing was needed or would work in "rich" Winter Park, we quickly realized that even there, families were struggling. Of course, we had no idea at the time that one pallet of food and one small step of obedience would lead to the establishment of a center that would help feed thousands of people each week in Central Florida.

". . . we had no idea at the time that one pallet of food and one small step of obedience would lead to the establishment of a center that would help feed thousands of people each week in Central Florida."

The distribution of that one pallet of food went so well and the people we served were so appreciative, that every Wednesday afternoon after that, we began picking up a pallet of food to distribute. Before Wednesday service each week, a faithful team of volunteers would meet at the church after work, sort the food, clean it, and put it into smaller bags for distribution. In the service, they would lead the congregation in prayer that God would use the distributed food to bring hope and help to children and families in need. We would put a small sign out on the road to let people in passing cars know that if they needed help, we were willing to serve them.

Each week, I was incredibly moved by the huge impact our small acts of kindness had on people who needed a little encouragement and hope. Tears would flow, people would hug, volunteers were touched, and good things were happening. It wasn't rocket science, but we seemed to be onto something.

Not long after this, our distribution program grew and we were out of room. We needed to find a campus we could grow into and expand our reach. It just so happened, a campus was available; an old church building sixteen miles away, in downtown Orlando. Though we were determined to live beyond ordinary, it would take an extraordinary effort to stay committed to our vision.

Downtown Orlando: A World Away

It took months of casting the vision for us to get buy-in from the church membership to take the huge leap of faith to move our church from the well-manicured suburbs of Winter Park to a decaying, run down, inner city area of Orlando, Florida. Even after the move, many people in the church questioned why we made such a drastic move to the inner city. At that time, people who could do so were leaving downtown Orlando in droves, moving to the suburbs. We were doing the exact opposite. It was quite a shock to the faith of many. So unusual was our decision that our local newspaper, the *Orlando Sentinel*, considered it front page news—headline worthy!

Though our move was unusual and difficult, I was confident it was the right move. Just months after the move, to all who were committed to our beyond ordinary vision, the reason we were led to make the move became clear. Hurting families in need began flooding into our church. We had never seen anything like it. Our church, Destiny, was living out its destiny and being pushed like never before to meet not just the needs of our congregation, but of the community around us as well.

A Hand Up, Not a Handout (Beyond Ordinary Approach)

To meet the needs of hurting families in need of food assistance and help, we knew we didn't want to duplicate what other churches and nonprofit centers were doing. Again, we wanted to go beyond ordinary. Most of the families that flocked to our church were not homeless. In fact, most of them were working families, with moms or dads who often worked two jobs, yet were still unable to make ends meet. These families were not asking for handouts. They wanted a hand up (#handup).

As I researched this, I found that many organizations and non-profit centers in our community applied a traditional model, and simply handed out food. Although this was admirable, it fostered an unhealthy entitlement attitude in many recipients that I found disillusioning. We needed a beyond ordinary approach, by which we invested our heart and resources into people and families that wanted to be empowered, not entitled; that were willing to be a part of the process and have "skin in the game." It was a radical approach and not widely accepted at the time, but one I felt strongly about pioneering. This model would build dignity and responsibility in people, so both donor and recipient would feel good about it.

"This model would build dignity and responsibility in people, so both donor and recipient would feel good about it."

Destiny Community Assistance Center Is Born

In the summer of 2001, we made plans to begin implementation of this innovative model of assistance. This beyond ordinary approach took months to fine-tune and develop, but we owe much to the Habitat for Humanity nonprofit model for our own. They did not simply give homes away to families in need, but partnered with them to work toward finding affordable housing. Poor working families had to apply themselves and expend considerable "sweat equity" toward the goal of home ownership. I remember thinking to myself, *If they can do this model with homes, why can't we use it with food?* We would not simply give food away all the time. We would develop a model by which working families in need would partner with us, and we would make affordable food available for purchase, helping move families from poverty to self-sustainability. (What we were setting out to do had never really been done before, and though we didn't realize it at the time, we were pioneering a model that would eventually be used all over the world.) The church members were on board and excited to launch this innovative model for our community, but we needed more than just passion and vision for our dream to become reality; we needed funding.

$10,000—All the Money in the World

I remember our breakthrough moment quite vividly. I had just delivered an emotional sermon, sharing with great passion and fervor the need for our church to do something bigger than us and start reaching out to needy families in our community like never before. In the sermon, I challenged members with the truth that the vision could only become reality with their prayer and financial support, and through their volunteer help.

My brother, Kris, one of my closest friends and a church member, came up to me in the church lobby and placed an envelope in my hand. He simply said, "Take this gift and let's make this thing happen." At the time, I didn't open the envelope, but simply thanked him. I put the envelope in my pocket and finished shaking hands and speaking with other members.

On the ride home, I was exhausted but very excited, encouraged by the response and comments of church members. It was obvious the church was willing to move forward with this ambitious project and we had the momentum for which we had been planning and praying. Little did I know, just minutes later, the momentum I sensed would spike to a whole new level.

Just after lunch, I remembered the envelope my brother had given me. I grabbed it out of my suit jacket pocket and nonchalantly opened it up. I was shocked. Not in a million years did I expect to see all those zero's behind that number one—four to be exact. I was holding a check for $10,000!

As a church made up of young adults (not known for large pocketbooks), that was by far the largest gift we had ever received. I was overcome with gratitude. That $10,000 was exactly what we needed to open the food pantry in downtown Orlando in

September 2001. I am forever grateful that God used my younger brother in such a wonderful way to catapult our dream into reality.

Keys to Living Beyond Ordinary

There is an application to you and your life in all this: God did not create you to be ordinary. He created you to live beyond ordinary. To live life beyond ordinary, you must be prayerfully alert and aware of your culture, surroundings, people, and events, and be ready to confidently respond to beyond ordinary opportunities with faith. Just as in our early days of starting a new nonprofit, what you see and how you react make all the difference.

"God did not create you to be ordinary. He created you to live beyond ordinary."

"If you change the way you look at things, the things you look at change."—Wayne Dyer

1. Look Outside (Observation, Motivation)

We miss so much around us simply because we are not watching and observing. Whether driving, walking, even running, it seems like everyone's attention today is focused on their smartphones. However, those who live beyond ordinary lives do not spend all their time looking at themselves and their own needs. They have learned to look outside themselves to the needs of those around them, get motivated by a vision of a need they can meet, and then act on meeting that need. They cannot help but serve by volunteering at a food bank, helping with the local Girl Scout troop, or volunteering with Big Brothers or the YMCA. They are predisposed to activity that brings hope and change.

Prayerfully look around to see all the needs in your community and you will be inspired to make a difference. Those who live beyond ordinary lives invest a great deal of time in looking outside and allowing themselves to be moved to act. As Bill Wilson, founder of the Metro World Child nonprofit has said, "The need is the call." This is true more often than not. However, to be moved, we must first allow ourselves to see and feel the need.

As a boy growing up in the church, I had trouble understanding why the church did not seem to have a passion for the poor like Jesus did. The church seemed to be more passionate about buildings, personalities, and programs than they did people—especially poor people. In my lifetime of ministry, I've always remembered the promise: "Go after the ones no one wants and God will bring you the ones everyone's after." I've never been motivated to go after the rich, powerful, and influential. As I focus on those in need—the poor and the hurting—I've noticed God has a way of causing people to cross my path who come alongside me to fulfill our part in His mission.

"Go after the ones no one wants and God will bring you the ones everyone's after."

There are things happening around you right now that need to be seen by you. It's no mistake that you are where you are at this time. No one else has the capacity or vision to see things the way you do and meet the need you will meet. You have been positioned in your neighborhood and community for this moment in time. Don't become so busy that you neglect to see what is around you. Stop, look around, get motivated by a need, act on meeting that need, and receive the blessing God holds for you.

2. Look Up (Inspiration)

Helping people in a beyond ordinary way is hard and not for the faint of heart. It can be frustrating when it seems the need never ends or the task is impossible. At times, people you help don't live up to their end of the bargain, and it hurts your heart. The war against poverty is all-out, all the time. You will need inspiration to maintain the courage and strength required to fight—to know you do not fight alone. I draw such inspiration from a personal relationship with Christ. He sustains me in living beyond ordinary.

David, the shepherd boy who would later become king, declared in Psalm 121:1 (NIV): "I lift up my eyes to the mountains—where does my help come from? My help comes from the Lord, the Maker of heaven and earth." David knew where his help came from, and was inspired to slay a giant and change the destiny of a nation. In times of stress, discouragement, and fear, I know I can look up and find peace, strength, and direction from Jesus, a source far more powerful than I will ever be.

Stop right now and ask yourself: *From where do I draw my inspiration?* When you look up, you discover true help and wisdom in your time of need. You hear and see things that many people do not.

Looking up helps me stay focused on things that really matter and gain insight I need to successfully lead. Though I did not grow up in a home that was familiar with poverty and the issues the poor face, I believe God inspired me to help and reach out, for these people are dear to His heart. He inspired me to live beyond ordinary.

3. Look Inside (Self-Evaluation)

What are you doing? Why are you doing it? Living beyond ordinary demands that you stop and look inside to evaluate and reevaluate what you are doing and why, to be sure you are staying true to your life's mission or vision and purpose. To live beyond ordinary, we must regularly inspect our lives, our hearts, and our motives. Self-evaluation is a necessary step to becoming the person you were meant to be.

My wife, Tammi, is a real estate appraiser. Her job is to look at and inspect every detail of a house, from its physical qualities (construction) and condition to other qualities that determine its value, such as the surrounding neighborhood. She takes great pride in this rigorous process of evaluation. Just as she spends

countless hours looking at every detail, we must also take sufficient time, energy, and focus to look into our own hearts and make
sure all is well. By looking inside, we see where we can refocus
and redirect. Our vision will become clear only after we look into
our heart and look outside our dreams. Whoever looks inside,
awakens.

**"Our vision will become clear only after we look into
our heart and look outside our dreams. Whoever
looks inside, awakens."**

The wisest of all men, Solomon, once said, "Catch for us the
foxes, the little foxes that ruin the vineyards" (Song of Songs 2:15,
NIV). Solomon knew that the big foxes were tall enough to eat the
fruit of the vine and caused little harm, but the small foxes were
not tall enough to reach the fruit, so they would eat the sprouts,
thus damaging the vines, keeping them from reaching their full
potential. Watch out for the seemingly insignificant things in your
life that steal life from you, seek to undermine your life's mission and purpose, and keep you from reaching your God-given
potential.

I find that the busyness of life can keep me from looking inside
and evaluating my heart, thoughts, and attitudes, so I must be
intentional about this. Along with my personal self-evaluation,
several times a month, as a ministry, we stop and ask tough questions of ourselves: we look inside. Such purposeful self-evaluation
forces us to ask tough questions, ensures the foundation is strong
and secure, and confirms we are on mission, heading in the right
direction, and fulfilling the vision.

4. Look Back (Reflection)

Two pieces of advice you will often hear people share are: "Don't
look back," and "Don't live in the past." Though I agree that living
in the past is not helpful, I strongly believe that from time to time,

it is helpful and necessary to take a look back. Certainly, we can recall lessons we've learned from past experiences and mistakes, to avoid repeating them. We can gain valuable insights from our history that help us move more boldly and ably into a future of living life beyond ordinary.

Steve Jobs learned the secret of looking back: "For the past 33 years, I have looked in the mirror every morning and asked myself: 'If today were the last day of my life, would I want to do what I am about to do today?' And whenever the answer has been 'no' for too many days in a row, I know I need to change something." As a ministry, to chart our course, we regularly look back at both things that did work and things that did not work. We are very honest about what is not working and changing it to make it work, if at all possible. We also make ourselves students of the track record of other nonprofits and ministries, to learn what did and did not work for them. In these ways, looking back helps us to make wise choices as we move ahead.

Ignoring problems will not make them go away. Those who would live beyond ordinary lives face their troubles or circumstance head on. They face them by looking at them with courage and boldness, and avoid the temptation to avoid or sidestep issues. To those facing troubles, James writes: "Consider it pure joy, my brothers and sisters, whenever you face trials of many kinds, because you know that the testing of your faith produces perseverance. Let perseverance finish its work so that you may be mature and complete, not lacking anything" (James 1:2-4, NIV). Consider for a moment the lessons you've learned from your past troubles and you will quickly see the truth of this.

Life is essentially a series of learning experiences, from beginning to end. Each experience, positive or negative, holds the potential to make us grow as Christlike people, even though this is sometimes hard to see or believe. One chief purpose of this world is to help us develop our character, and part of that development comes from tests and trials we endure as we march forward. You have been through seasons of joy and sorrow. Your past can serve as a great guide to living a future beyond ordinary, if you take time to reflect on it, learn from it, and grow because of it.

Esther . . . Anything but Ordinary

"I was not a messiah, but an ordinary man who had become a leader because of extraordinary circumstances."—Nelson Mandela

The Bible heroine, Esther, did not start out as a proven leader. She was not born to privilege or wealth—quite the contrary. Esther was an outcast, an orphan who was adopted, but ultimately raised on the wrong side of the tracks. (Her story is found in the Old Testament book of Esther.) Though some take issue with the book of Esther because the word, "God," cannot be found in it, I contend the DNA of God is found throughout this fascinating story of a girl rejected by men but chosen by God to live a beyond ordinary life.

Esther, a Jew, was discovered by the king and elevated to a royal position at a very critical time. At the time, one of the king's respected officials, Haman, had proposed and received the king's approval for a persecution of the Jews, in general, and death to Esther's uncle, Mordecai, in particular. Mordecai "texted" an urgent appeal to Esther: "Don't think that just because you live in the king's house you're the one Jew who will get out of this alive. If you persist in staying silent at a time like this, help and deliverance will arrive for the Jews from someplace else; but you and your family will be wiped out. Who knows? Maybe you were made queen for just such a time as this" (Esther 4:12-14, MSG).

This was a historic moment; a turning point for Esther. She didn't see it coming; it just happened. If she would be willing to risk her life to save the Jewish people from destruction, she would move beyond ordinary and become extraordinary. She would never be the same. Her response is one that still inspires countless millions, even thousands of years later, reflecting her inner beauty: "I'll go to the king, even though it's forbidden. If I die, I die" (Esther 4:16, MSG).

Esther was ready and willing to embrace even death in order to obey God's call and vision for her life, and so was able to find her place among those who live beyond ordinary lives.

In Jewish culture, the name "Esther" means, "shining star." At one of the darkest moments in Jewish history, God used this innocent, formerly rejected and lonely girl, to bring light and freedom to an entire generation. Esther was just an ordinary person who became a beyond ordinary leader, due to extraordinary circumstances. In fact, to this day, the Jewish people celebrate a holiday commemorating the deliverance of the Jewish people, due to Esther's beyond ordinary action.

Esther's shining example in the darkest of times should inspire us to seek our own opportunity to move beyond ordinary. You were created for a time such as this, for a unique purpose that only you can live. As you pursue this opportunity and live it out, you will move beyond ordinary to extraordinary. You will never be the same.

Use your smartphone or tablet QR code reader to watch an important video about beyond ordinary living! Or, enter this link in your web browser: www.livingbeyondordinary.org/videos/chapter1.

Tweet these!

How are you living beyond ordinary? #LivingBeyondOrdinary http://bit.ly/1pVu3o1

How are you helping others with a hand up? #handup http://bit.ly/1pVu3o1

"The only thing we have to fear is fear itself."
—Franklin D. Roosevelt

~

"I have learned over the years that when one's mind is made up, this diminishes fear; knowing what must be done does away with fear."—Rosa Parks

~

"It is the strange fate of man, that even in the greatest of evils the fear of the worst continues to haunt him."
—Johann Wolfgang von Goethe

~

"We fear things in proportion to our ignorance of them."
—Christian Nestell Bovee

~

"There is no passion so contagious as that of fear."
—Michel de Montaigne

~

"Only when we are no longer afraid do we begin to live."
—Dorothy Thompson

~

CHAPTER 2

THE JOURNEY BEYOND ORDINARY LIVING

Lisa was a single mom from Miami with one child, a small five-year-old daughter named Samantha. She worked as a waitress and struggled each day to make life work. Trapped in an abusive relationship, Samantha lived in fear for her life and the life of her daughter. The man she loved said he loved her, but it was clear he loved drinking much more. When he "got to drinking," a nightmare of terror would ensue for Samantha and her daughter. Each day became a life and death struggle. Battered and bruised, her only goal each day was to survive and make it through to the next day—where the pain and abuse would start all over again.

Uncertain Times . . . Unlimited Opportunity

One night, in desperation and despair, clinging to the smallest sliver of hope and a mustard seed of faith in God, Lisa made a decision that would change her life: She would face her greatest fear, move out, and move on with her life. There had to be more to life than shame, guilt, and abuse. Stealthily, she packed up her life's meager belongings, filled her car's tank with gas, took her daughter by the hand, and fled north. She had no idea where she was going or where she would end up; she just knew it was time to move beyond the bleak life she had been living to find a life beyond abuse and pain.

Hours later, Lisa found herself in south Orlando; full of hope, but out of gas. She pulled into our campus at 150 West Michigan Street, not knowing who we were or what we did. She just saw the lighted parking lot and, with no other options, coasted in on fumes. This precious young woman and her daughter spent the night in their car. Lisa grew anxious about what daylight would bring and found only a restless sleep that night.

When Lisa awoke, she noticed the parking lot was full and saw many families entering our building. She finally mustered the courage to walk inside, simply to ask for directions to a place where she could get help. Little did she know, her faith had led her to a place of hope and help! Within a few hours, she would secure long-term housing, be directed to a program for domestic violence survivors, find a school for her daughter, and eventually secure an entry-level job with us there at CFOC (Community Food and Outreach Center). With her life at its lowest ebb, with nowhere else to turn, Lisa had found more than a hand up in helping secure a job and place to live: She had found hope and a new start in life.

Lisa's story is just one of many I could share, for we have been able to serve tens of thousands in our quest to live beyond ordinary lives, as we pour ourselves out in love to those in need.

Small Steps toward a Big Dream

Looking back, that $10,000 gift from Kris enabled us to establish ourselves there on Michigan Street for Lisa and thousands of others to find. It had given us the ability to look at potential warehouses we could lease to accomplish our mission. After months of searching, we had finally decided on that venue on Michigan Street, just a few blocks from our church on Orange Avenue. At the time, I didn't realize the significance of the street name that divided Michigan Street, which was Division Avenue. Only as we got serious about the property did a little research find that years before, city leaders had named the street "Division" because it marked a clear division in Orlando between the haves and the have-nots. This street was to serve as a barrier between the rich and the poor, and sadly typical of the time, separate Blacks from Whites. The building was very close to the railroad line that ran through downtown Orlando. How ironic that we would pick a location for a food pantry in downtown Orlando that had histori-cally served as a dividing line between the races, as we would now break through that barrier to offer hope and help to families of all colors.

In the summer of 2001, the building was secured and we began to prepare it, cleaning it up and filling it with shelves, office equipment, and most importantly, food. Each Saturday, volunteer groups, youth groups, friends, and our families worked around the clock to get the building ready. We hired our first staff person and pastor to oversee the project and quickly reached out to city lead-ers, nonprofit leaders, and the general public to let everyone know about the new nonprofit we were opening, and our vision for ben-efitting our community. The excitement was building and prepara-tions were coming along very nicely. All the pieces were falling into place seamlessly. Our staff began to discuss opening day.

Originally, we discussed Tuesday, September 11, 2001, as our grand opening day. However, after some thought, the staff decided we needed to do a soft opening and take a few days to get ready, so we landed on September 1, 2001, as the official first day of opera-tion. We were a small church that had taken on a big project, but we were optimistic about the future. Optimistic, that is, until some-thing happened that would threaten everything we were doing.

9/11: A Day of Destiny

You probably remember exactly where you were and what you were doing when you heard about the attacks on September 11,

2001. I was in a staff meeting at the church, discussing—among other things—the great stories and success of our then ten-day-old food pantry. We seemed to have worked out all the kinks and were feeling pretty good and confident that we had the thing figured out. We were delighted and encouraged by the stories of families being helped and the progress being made just a few blocks away from our church building, at CFOC (Destiny Community Assistance Center, at the time). A dedicated staff person, Walter Gamb, interrupted our meeting and simply said: "Pastor Scott, we have a national tragedy unfolding in New York City. You may want to turn on the television to see what is happening." We abruptly canceled the meeting and the staff moved to the nearest TV to see for themselves the impact of the terrorist attacks on the twin towers of the World Trade Center. We had no idea then that the ripple effect of one of the greatest national tragedies in our country's short history would change our world, shake Central Florida to its core, and forever change our mission in downtown Orlando.

For the first few hours that day, I was glued to the television set in my office. I just couldn't believe what I was seeing. Sadness and grief raced through my mind and body, and I was struck numb and left in shock at what I was seeing and hearing. I just couldn't believe it. For the rest of that day, like millions of Americans, I had to sort this all out in my heart and mind. *How would I explain this to my four young children? How would I address this tragedy with the church family? How would I respond as a community leader?* For several hours, I wrestled with these questions. It seemed that with each passing moment, new questions arose, and I remember feeling very angry and confused. Hopelessness started to creep into my mind.

"What are we going to do?"

It wasn't until a few days later that the most impactful question came. In a conversation with a church leader about the attacks and the crisis that followed, he asked me: "What are we going to do about all the families that are about to lose their jobs because of this?" In the midst of all the emotion, anger, and confusion, the real impact the attacks would have on our nation, state, city, and our new small new pantry, had not dawned on me.

The challenge we faced had already been daunting. Central Florida is known worldwide as a key vacation destination, featuring world-class theme park attractions: Disney World, Sea World, Universal Studios, and so much more. There are tens of thousands of service and tourism jobs here, but the pay is low, making it very difficult for families to survive financially, especially given the state of the economy over the last several years. In fact, I heard recently that Central Florida led the nation in one key income tier: 37 percent of our workforce (around 400,000 people) makes under $25,000 a year. Because of these economic realities, our model for serving the poor and providing assistance for the working poor was perfectly suited for our region, and the timing for the establishment of our center could not have been better. I recalled that initially, it had taken months for the vision of the Destiny Community Assistance Center to take hold in the hearts of our members, but they were on fire for it now. Still, we were all about to grow up very fast.

Though I had not considered how 9/11 would shape our little nonprofit and thrust it into a new level for which we were not really prepared, even in the face of sorrow and pain, I had to respond with boldness and confidence. It was a bit overwhelming, but I knew we were ready for a beyond ordinary start (#LivingBeyondOrdinary).

Overcoming Fear of the Unknown on the Journey to Living Beyond Ordinary

The nature of life is change, growth, and the exploration of new horizons. Change is the only constant in life, some have wryly noted. It is happening all around us, and if we are growing, it is happening in us. For those fully alive, change is here to stay.

Embrace Change and Reject the Comfort Zone

If we are to truly and fully live life, we will never be allowed to remain in our comfort zone for long, for growth is always uncomfortable. We wrongly believe that true security is found in hanging on to what makes us comfortable, but comfort is actually our enemy, and living within our comfort zones can make our lives dull, boring, and less than ordinary. True security is actually found in embracing the very things that cause us to live by faith. We should always make choices that put us against our comfort zone. To live beyond ordinary lives, we must move beyond the fear of the new and unknown and, in faith, embrace uncomfortable change (#fearlessliving).

"To live beyond ordinary lives, we must move beyond the fear of the new and unknown and, in faith, embrace uncomfortable change (#fearlessliving)."

Refuse to Camp Out on Success

The biggest enemy of exceeding greatness, world-class innovation, and exponential growth is often . . . success. Whether in our personal or professional lives, success can be intoxicating . . . and deadly. In fact, once their goals are actualized, many people become confused and disoriented, unsure of what to do next, resting on their laurels, lulled into inactivity and stagnation. Those who would live beyond ordinary lives consider success to be simply one more rung on a lifelong upward trajectory to grow and become all they were destined to be.

Value Failure

Many people so fear failure that they avoid all risk, resist change, refuse to learn or do new things, and remain safely within their comfort zone. Essentially, they live life in a small box. They do not understand that life is designed to be an adventure—a learning experience—and that failure is not fatal (even though it may feel that way, at times). Outside the box, though it is true we may fall from time to time, it is also true that any fall can be a fall forward. As Henry Ford said, "Failure is simply the opportunity to begin again, this time more intelligently." When confronted with failure, we should ask ourselves, "What can I learn from this failure to fall forward?" Those who would live beyond ordinary lives embrace the lessons of failure and learn, over time, that the fear of failure diminishes with each step of success.

Look Boldly to the Future

No one is guaranteed the next year, month, day, hour, or even the next minute. All of us have an uncertainty about the future. We must all learn from the past (without living in it or regretting it), live confidently in the present, and fearlessly face the unknown, uncertain future with optimism. The pessimist who believes things will only grow worse loses hope, gives in to the paralysis of fear, perpetually dwells in the problem, and ultimately loses all energy to be part of the solution. Those who would live beyond ordinary lives are led by a bright, optimistic vision of all the future could be and find unlimited resources within and around them to make that vision a reality.

Jim Morrison, lead singer of the Doors, once said, "There are things known and things unknown, and in between are the doors." Between the known and the unknown are the doors of life. Those who would live beyond ordinary lives are not fearful of the unknown. They embrace things that are hidden, with confidence, courage, and certainty, though uncertain and unfamiliar.

Venture out and live by faith. None of us enjoys a completely mapped out future, with every question answered and concern addressed before we proceed. Life does not give us a crystal ball we can simply look into to get a clear vision of the future. Life is wildly unpredictable, and our future will always hold adventure, requiring us to move ahead, led by what we cannot touch or feel.

The life of faith requires us to walk in confidence and courage, even as others look for the tangible to hold onto.

Fear cries for us to stay in the seeable and predictable. Faith cries out for us to venture into the deep and unknown. Faith tells us to take the unfamiliar path, for that path is filled with wonder and surprise. Those who would live beyond ordinary thrive on the unfamiliar and live by faith, not by sight.

"Fear cries for us to stay in the seeable and predictable. Faith cries out for us to venture into the deep and unknown."

In a Box Called a Boat

Comfort zones, fear, past success, resistance to change and growth—all of these can make our lives small, dull, ordinary, and lifeless; like living in a box. Boxes confine. Boxes limit. Boxes constrict. If we are to walk on this journey to live beyond ordinary, we must live by faith and not allow ourselves to be limited by our fears (#noboundaries).

One story in the New Testament, of Jesus and Peter, illustrates how to walk by faith and not allow our fears to limit us or box us in:

> Immediately Jesus made the disciples get into the boat and go on ahead of him to the other side, while he dismissed the crowd. After he had dismissed them, he went up on a mountainside by himself to pray. Later that night, he was there alone, and the boat was already a considerable distance from land, buffeted by the waves because the wind was against it.
>
> Shortly before dawn Jesus went out to them, walking on the lake. When the disciples saw him walking on the

lake, they were terrified. "It's a ghost," they said, and cried out in fear.

But Jesus immediately said to them: "Take courage! It is I. Don't be afraid."

"Lord, if it's you," Peter replied, "tell me to come to you on the water."

"Come," he said.

Then Peter got down out of the boat, walked on the water and came toward Jesus. But when he saw the wind, he was afraid and, beginning to sink, cried out, "Lord, save me!"

Immediately Jesus reached out his hand and caught him. "You of little faith," he said, "why did you doubt?" (Matthew 14:22-31, NIV)

Peter was in a boat, but think of it as a box—a limiting, confining wooden box on water that brought a sense of security and comfort. Although Peter wanted to get out of the boat box and walk on water to get to Christ, he fought a battle that we all face on a daily basis—the fight between faith and fear. However, unlike many of us, Peter made the courageous decision to get out of his box. Even though once he started to experience his walk of faith, he saw the wind and waves and quickly fell back into doubt and fear, the fact is, he walked on water, doing something he had never done before, personally experiencing God's miraculous power like never before.

If we don't master our fears, our fears will master us and keep us enclosed and entrapped—in a box. We all have to make the choice that Peter ultimately made: Allow our fears to keep us ensnared, or walk by faith and venture out of the box and into a new life experience, with confidence and power. As we do this each day, we will live a life beyond ordinary.

Use your smartphone or tablet QR code reader to watch an important video about beyond ordinary living! Or, enter this link in your web browser: www.livingbeyondordinary.org/videos/chapter2.

Tweet these!

What fear are you overcoming to live beyond ordinary? #fearlessliving http://bit.ly/1pVu3o1

What is holding you back from living beyond ordinary? #noboundaries http://bit.ly/1pVu3o1

"It is easier to forgive an enemy than to forgive a friend."
—William Blake

~

"Is it possible to succeed without any act of betrayal?"
—Jean Renoir

~

"It's hard to tell who has your back, from who has it long enough just to stab you in it . . ."—Nicole Richie

~

"But I say unto you, love your enemies, and pray for them that persecute you; that ye may be sons of your Father who is in heaven: for he maketh his sun to rise on the evil and the good, and sendeth rain on the just and the unjust."—Jesus Christ (Matthew 5:44-45, ASV)

~

"We must develop and maintain the capacity to forgive. He who is devoid of the power to forgive is devoid of the power to love. There is some good in the worst of us and some evil in the best of us. When we discover this, we are less prone to hate our enemies."
—Dr. Martin Luther King, Jr.

~

"You have enemies? Good. That means you've stood up for something, sometime in your life."—Winston Churchill

~

"If you want to make enemies, try to change something."
—Woodrow Wilson

~

CHAPTER 3

ENEMIES OF BEYOND ORDINARY LIVING

I remember the moment like it was yesterday. It was a very busy day, packed with activity and meetings. In the midst of that flurry of activity, the call came in and went to my voicemail. The message was brief, polite, yet to the point: "Our media reporter will be at your campus at 3 p.m. to complete our investigation."

Complete the investigation?

My initial reaction was shock and dismay. I couldn't figure out what they meant by "investigation," but I let them know I would be available to talk with them. I pulled a few members of my staff together to see if there was anything I was unaware of, to try and figure out what was going on. I also called a few board members and let them know what was going on. Armed with limited information, we tried our best to be prepared. However, the message from the media outlet was so vague, it made it very difficult for us to prepare.

Under Investigation: Friendly Fire
by Unfriendly Enemies

The reporter showed up at the outreach center at 3 p.m., on the dot. A staff person opened my office door to let me know, and I asked her to let the reporter in. From the minute I began talking with the reporter, I sensed that the verdict was already in. The reporter had clearly already made up his mind that we were guilty of wrongdoing. The reporter started our conversation with a few inflammatory, accusatory comments that really took me by surprise. I was quickly overwhelmed, disgusted, and desperately tried to maintain my composure.

The reporter's first comment had been that there was an investigation into our charity. I politely asked him who was conducting the investigation and how long it had been going on. He responded: "Our media outlet decided to launch the investigation just this morning, so it started at 10 a.m. We are making our findings public tonight."

I thought to myself, *What gives them the right to randomly investigate us, and what kind of investigation goes public after only six hours of research?* I have since learned that the word "investigation" may have an altogether different meaning for the media than it would for you and I. In many cases, the reporter is given a story or issue to investigate at a morning meeting and, due to nightly news deadlines, has only a few hours to research and investigate it before going to air or press, or posting it online. I'm not sure I agree with this, but that's the way it goes. Sometimes life isn't fair. And as far as I was concerned, the investigation was not fair, and things began going downhill fast.

The second comment the reporter made to me was equally shocking and disappointing. Just prior to the interview, he disclosed that he had just come from another nonprofit to get a comment on the investigation from one of their leaders—the same nonprofit that had contacted the media outlet, provoking the initial investigation. This nonprofit was one of a few that had opposed us from the start because they considered us a threat and wanted to keep doing things the way they had "always" been done, and protect the status quo. In short, they had thrown us under the bus. We were still very young, and sure, we had made some mistakes, but we were making a big splash in our community. Every day, hundreds of people were receiving help from us and we were gaining momentum. They were threatened by our success, so they positioned themselves as our enemies. (This is just one of the reasons starting a nonprofit from ground zero is very difficult and not for the faint of heart.)

Just before the recorded interview, the reporter said, "You'll be OK after this report. It will sting for a few weeks, but you'll survive and be better for it." I thought that was an interesting comment to make at the start of a supposedly objective interview.

The Interview and Accusation

The interview basically centered on the issue that our charity embraced (and still embraces), a then new and innovative model: "Provide a hand up, not a hand out." The other nonprofit had vilified us, accusing us of merely selling food to the poor. Though it was true we did ask the working poor families we served to give the outreach a small donation for the food they received, we did so in order to help them participate in their long process toward self-sustainability. We did this in the context of the relationship we had developed with them. In the interview, I explained how our model celebrates the fact that entitlement doesn't work, but empowerment does. I went on to say that when we partner with families in need, and ask them to be accountable and partner with us, it builds dignity and accountability. After that, the reporter quickly packed up and left.

I wish I could tell you that this entire traumatic event blew over in a day and that the story ended there. Sadly, the interview and story made headline news later that evening.

Things got worse.

It turned out, the media report was only one part of a strategic plot by that adversarial nonprofit to close us down. The same day the story ran, they also called the health inspector of our county. Within a few minutes, the health inspector found a few issues in our warehouse (unrelated to the media story), and suddenly our charity was closed down for three days. It was devastating, to say the least. Our staff was confused and disheartened, and we had to turn away from our doors many families and children in need. People already without hope, who had come to our campus for help, found us closed. Those three days were the longest and loneliest of my life.

Persistence Pays Off

In my mind, it was necessary to confront the General Manager (GM) of the media outlet that had run the negative story about us, especially since my credibility was at stake. I made an appointment with the GM of the media outlet. I brought along an outreach board member who was also an attorney. After a few minutes of customary small talk, I let the GM know how I felt about the whole situation, my displeasure with their so-called "investigation," my disappointment in the story they had run, and how their misrepresentations had affected the poor people of our community. After a few minutes of my near rant, I was shocked and surprised to find that the GM was unaware of the story—even though it had been his outlet's headline story a few days in a row. He may have been playing unaware as a ploy, but he genuinely did not seem to know any of the details—not even that the reporter I named was handling the story. The meeting ended very positively. The GM said he would look into it and do some research.

A few days after our meeting, I received a call from the media outlet. My first reaction was: "Oh, no. Here we go again!" However, to my surprise, the call was from a reporter who wanted to do a positive story on us. He wanted to set up an interview (amazing, to say the least). The interview went well, and a positive, uplifting story resulted from it.

I learned a few things over the years that applied throughout this situation, but one of the most important is this: A good name must be defended. Also, we must always stand for what is true, good, and right. I have also learned that persistence is vital for success. I am also quick to say, even years later, that I am so grateful for the media and all the good they do for society.

"You'll be better for it . . ."

After many years of evaluation and reflection on this traumatic time for our outreach, I came to recognize the truth of what the reporter told me just before the initial interview: "You'll be better for it." Now that I can view this drama in my rearview mirror, I can honestly say that the outreach is better for it—that I am better for it. Thankfully, we survived and became better, not bitter.

That's what enemies and critics can do for us, if we respond to them with character and integrity. Even the evil they intend for us can be turned around to work for our good. In now our thirteenth year of existence, this was the one and only time something like this happened. Although I wouldn't wish an attack like we endured on even my worst enemy, I learned a few things and became better for it.

Another Happy Ending

A few years later, ironically, I learned I would receive the Orange County Health Department Healthy Hero award. It was a very nice award and I enjoyed the recognition for what our staff had accomplished. The award and the banquet and ceremony were nice gestures, and I humbled by it all.

After the event, a gentleman approached me, said he was so very happy to see me, and asked to speak to me. Although I wasn't sure I knew him, as he started to speak, I realized he was the health inspector who had shut us down during our "learning experience." Face-to-face with me, with a tear in his eye, he whispered something I'll never forget. He said he hated closing our campus down as he had those years before, but explained he had been pressured to do so by local and state officials. He wanted me to know how incredibly happy he was to see our organization rise above and move forward, with character and integrity.

I am reminded of a reporter interviewing a man on his 100th birthday, asking, "What are you most proud of?"

"Well," said the old man, pondering the question. "I don't have an enemy in the world."

"That's quite an achievement!" said the reporter.

"Yep," added the old man. "I've outlived every last one of them."

When you determine to live a life beyond ordinary, you will have enemies. The idea is to "outlive" them (#LivingBeyond Ordinary).

"When you determine to live a life beyond ordinary, you will have enemies. The idea is to "outlive" them (#LivingBeyondOrdinary)."

Enemy Attitudes

Sometimes our biggest enemies are our own attitudes, or those of the people around us. The most common are the enemies of status quo, average, complacency, and compromise (#enemies).

The Enemy of Status Quo

The status quo is a formidable force in our society. That is, most people are content with things just the way they are. Their favorite six-word phrase is, "We've always done it this way." To them, change is a four-letter word. Those who would live beyond ordinary do not accept the status quo . . . they challenge it. Warren G. Bennies said, "The manager accepts the status quo; the leader challenges it." Every day, you and I will have to battle the force of the "same old, same old." As Gerry Adams says, "It will always be a battle a day between those who want maximum change and those who want to maintain the status quo." We need to live our lives with a passion to fight the forces of status quo.

The Enemy Called Average

No one wakes up and says to themselves, "Today, I want to be average," yet in today's society, there is tremendous pressure to fit in and simply be average. Average is one of the greatest enemies we will ever face. Don't allow average to make you mediocre and bland. John Mason says, "You were born an original, don't die a copy."

The Enemy Called Complacency

Jimmy Carter once said, "I hate to see complacency prevail in our lives when it's so directly contrary to the teaching of Christ." Complacency is being satisfied with how things are, and being unwilling to make them better. Those who would live beyond ordinary lives position themselves in situations that make them venture out, expanding their horizons and increasing their vision. Trent Reznor says it this way: "I really try to put myself in uncomfortable situations. Complacency is my enemy."

The Enemy Called Compromise

In our pursuit of living beyond ordinary, we will always be faced with the temptation to compromise our character, values, and beliefs, usually with promises of an easier way, or needed funds or help. Small compromises here and there soon become grave threats to all the good we have done. "Courage, not compromise, brings the smile of God's approval," wrote Thomas S. Monson. We must be determined to fight this foe with abandon whenever it raises its ugly head. The approval of God and man are best experienced when we live lives free from compromise and full of courage and conviction (#breakingfree).

Things Those Who Live Beyond Ordinary Lives Know About Enemies

There are quite a number of things those who live beyond ordinary have learned about enemies.

Enemies Will Not Magically Disappear on Their Own

How wonderful would it be to go to bed at night and wake up the next morning to find our enemies gone? Unfortunately, it just doesn't work like that, and it never will. We can't simply stick our heads in the sand and hope that the voice of the enemy we are facing will be gone. One of the toughest lessons in life for all of us is learning how to manage our enemies. James 1:2 says, "Consider it pure joy, my brothers and sisters, whenever you face trials of many kinds" (NIV). I love the challenge James gives us to face our trails. Running from them won't work. Hoping they won't resurface doesn't work either. I challenge you to step up and face them head on. You'll find that when you determine to boldly face them, you will find the strength you need to do so.

Enemies Get Bigger the Longer You Leave Them Alone

The more we leave our enemies alone and fail to confront them, the bigger and more powerful they become. If you knew termites had infested your home, you would make it a high priority to address the issue right away, because termite infestations only grow worse as you leave them alone. By leaving enemies alone you empower them. They are emboldened and become an even stronger force down the road. You need to come up with your game plan and work to resolve their issues with you, if possible.

Enemies Attract Enemies

Your enemies will have the unique ability to attract others who think similarly to the way they do. They tend to run in groups, thriving on the negative energy that can be found in numbers. They all seem to come out at the same time and attack when you are most vulnerable. That's why the best approach is to be proactive and fight them head on.

Enemies Attack the Young

The plan of the enemy has been, and always will be, to attack us when we are young, and to attack our dreams when they are newly birthed and most vulnerable. Expect attacks and nonconstructive criticism when your dream is small and can easily become prey.

I have four children. Each one of them, when they were babies, were weak and unable to fight for themselves. However, as they grew year by year, they became stronger and more able to defend themselves. Be careful in the early stages of your dream. Make sure you are able to defend it with wisdom and courage.

Enemies Are Opportunists

The enemies we face every day are looking for an open window to attack. In their conversations, emails, texts, and meetings, they are on the hunt for ways to attack and discredit, rarely offering constructive feedback and encouragement (if ever). It seems to be the way they are wired. They can't seem to help it! They are looking for an opportunity to cause drama and conflict. It is important to deny them such opportunities and only allow into your vision those who share it, who are fair and balanced, and who are people of character and integrity.

Judas: Betrayal with a Kiss

Betrayal is as old as life itself. History holds countless stories of betrayal over the centuries. Even Jesus, the most visionary leader of the greatest nonprofit of all time, had to deal with enemies. His greatest enemies were the religious leaders of His day. Still, He understood His fight was not with sinners; He loved them. His fight was with the religious leaders and their hypocrisy. In addition to fighting the religious leaders, He also had to deal with an enemy within His inner circle of disciples who supposedly shared His vision, heart, and mission: Judas.

"Even Jesus, the most visionary leader of the greatest nonprofit of all time, had to deal with enemies."

> Then one of the Twelve—the one called Judas Iscariot—went to the chief priests and asked, "What are you willing to give me if I deliver him over to you?" So they counted out for him thirty pieces of silver. 16 From then on Judas watched for an opportunity to hand him over. (Matthew 26:14-16, NIV)

> While he was still speaking, Judas, one of the Twelve, arrived. With him was a large crowd armed with swords and clubs, sent from the chief priests and the elders of the people. Now the betrayer had arranged a signal with them: "The one I kiss is the man; arrest him." Going at once to Jesus, Judas said, "Greetings, Rabbi!" and kissed him. Jesus replied, "Do what you came for, friend." Then the men stepped forward, seized Jesus and arrested him. (Matthew 26:47-50, NIV)

Only inches from the face of his own betrayer, Jesus looked at him and said, "Do what you came for, friend" (Matthew 26:50, NIV).

The husband betrayed by his wife. The employee passed over for a promotion promised by her employer. The secret between friends brought to light for all to see. A parent breaks a promise to his or her child. Family members turn on other family members, coworkers turn on coworkers, and friends betray friends. All of these are forms of betrayal—abandonments or violations of trust by someone close to us. Perhaps nothing makes us feel worse or shakes us to our core more than betrayal. We might even feel our world is falling apart. William Blake has written, "It is easier to forgive an enemy than to forgive a friend."

Most of us are confronted by enemies on a regular basis—even a Judas or two within the organizations we serve. Sometimes, we find out about them in the most public of ways—through gossip, the legal system, or the media—which only adds exponentially to the already great pain and hurt. Just imagine how Jesus must have felt when Judas, a close friend who traveled with Him, betrayed Him with a kiss.

Dealing with a Judas

1. Accept the fact that everyone, including you, will have a Judas (even someone who may be close to you).

Most people try to navigate through life "enemy free." They believe that the best way to live their lives is by doing everything necessary to avoid controversy and making enemies. I hate to burst their bubble, but no matter how hard they try, they will have enemies. As long as they are breathing, they will have enemies. You must accept the hard fact that you have enemies. The sooner you embrace this, the closer you will be to victory.

My grandfather used to tell me, "If you want to avoid controversy and making enemies, say nothing, do nothing, and be nothing." Life is full of people you will never please. It is impossible to walk through this life without critics and naysayers. I've found that people who try to please everyone end up unhappy, unfulfilled, and unsettled. They worry constantly about what other people think, and never accomplish anything.

When you realize you have enemies, it doesn't mean you have done anything wrong. In fact, it probably means you're doing something right. Enemies are proof that you are on the right track. If you are strolling through life without opposition, I would question if you're on the right road! The next time you experience opposition from enemies over who you are or what you are doing, shift your thinking from *Oh no* to *Oh yes:*

~ *Oh yes!* I'm making an impact.

~ *Oh yes!* I'm on the right track.

~ *Oh yes!* People are noticing my contributions.

~ *Oh yes!* I'm living beyond ordinary.

"My grandfather used to tell me, "If you want to avoid controversy and making enemies, say nothing, do nothing, and be nothing.""

Jesus picked twelve disciples, and one of them turned out to be an enemy—a betrayer. If Christ had enemies close by, so will you. It could be a coworker, church member, a member of your field or profession, or even a friend or family member. Don't become paranoid about this, but do develop a deeper awareness of the proximity of your Judas. Write the name (or initials) of your Judas (or two) here: _____.

2. Remember that often Judas doesn't really know what he is doing.

When dealing with difficult people and enemies, it is helpful to remind ourselves that many times, our Judas does not know what he or she is doing. Though they may seem sophisticated and deliberate in their attacks, often they do not fully know what they are doing. A few days after Jesus' confrontation with Judas, in His last moments on earth, He prayed a very powerful prayer that included this: "Father, forgive them, for they do not know what they are doing" (Luke 23:34, NIV). This is a powerful lesson for us all.

3. Remind yourself that the attack is against your mission, not you.

Judas was out to abort the mission of Christ. I believe that Jesus understood that Judas' attack was missional, not personal. Your Judas is attacking your mission—the calling on your life. It certainly may feel personal, but simply take a step back and take a long hard look, and you will soon discover that really, your mission is under attack.

4. Keep in mind that money is usually the motivation for betrayal.

Thirty pieces of silver. This is what the religious leaders in this story paid Judas for his betrayal of Jesus. They even called it "blood money." Though money is not the basis for every situation we face with our enemies, I would venture to say that many of the issues we confront will come down to money in one way or another. That's why Paul writes, "The love of money is a root of all kinds of evil" (1 Timothy 6:10, NIV).

5. Be aware that Judas will usually self-destruct.

I think that deep down; Jesus knew how the story would end for Judas. It would not be pretty. Most times, when our enemies make a life of betrayal, pain, and drama, their end is not usually a very good one. In Judas' case, it ended with him taking his own life. That's certainly the exception when it comes to our enemies, but I've found that people who make it their life ambition to cause trouble, strife, and drama usually end up paying a tremendous price for their folly.

6. Convince yourself that retaliation is not the best approach.

When Judas showed up in the garden with the authorities who meant to arrest Jesus, His friends—fresh from sleep—pulled out their swords and started to swing. I believe that often, our first reaction to an attack is to go for the sword and fight back. Though rewarding in the moment, such reactions only make these situations worse. After Peter cut off the ear of one of the soldiers, Jesus commanded His disciples to sheath their weapons and healed the soldier. In the moment, Peter likely felt that what he had done was right and good: Jesus knew a better way.

"I've found that people who make it their life ambition to cause trouble, strife, and drama usually end up paying a tremendous price for their folly."

---

7. Understand that only prayer can get you through the pain of betrayal.

Prayer is vital for overcoming betrayal and pain. Jesus happened to be in the Garden of Gethsemane, praying with His disciples, when Judas and Jesus' other enemies showed up. In the original Greek text, the word, "Gethsemane," means "olive press." Huge olive trees in the garden surrounded Jesus and His disciples. I've been to Israel many times, and it is amazing how big these trees are. When squeezed or pressed, the olives from these trees produce precious olive oil. Similarly, when our enemies betray us—squeezing us—whatever is inside us comes out. Jesus was fully equipped to face Judas' betrayal with peace and godly character because He had taken time to pray and meditate before it happened.

Pause for a moment here and pray for the battle you are in, and the Judas you named above. Ask God for help and strength. It never hurts to ask for help in difficult times. You'll find that you will respond much better to the enemies in your life if you simply pray before you battle.

8. Accept the principle that the best approach is forgiveness.

"Father, forgive them" (Luke 23:34, NIV) were some of the last words Jesus spoke on this earth. These powerful, liberating, yet very simple words can help us today as we deal with the pain of betrayal. Take a minute right now and speak them in regard to the Judas you named above: "Father, forgive him/her." Throughout my life, I have been amazed at the power of these words as I walked through painful times. I am sure you will feel this, too.

This message on the wall of Mother Teresa's home for children, in Calcutta, is one for all of us to embrace and internalize:

People are often unreasonable, irrational, and self-centered.
Forgive them anyway.
If you are kind, people may accuse you of selfish, ulterior motives.
Be kind anyway.
If you are successful, you will win some unfaithful friends and some genuine enemies. Succeed anyway.
If you are honest and sincere, people may deceive you.
Be honest and sincere anyway.
What you spend years creating, others could destroy overnight.
Create anyway.
If you find serenity and happiness, some may be jealous.
Be happy anyway.
The good you do today will often be forgotten.
Do good anyway.
Give the best you have, and it will never be enough.
Give your best anyway.
In the final analysis, it is between you and God. It was never between you and them anyway.
Peace on earth goodwill toward all men.[1]

Historically, December is a great time of year, when most people seem to be happiest and most generous. For me, this beautiful time of year begins with the Christmas story, when angels appeared to the shepherds and said, "Glory to God in the highest, and on earth peace, goodwill toward men!" (Luke 2:14, NKJV). I have come to use this verse as a guide. There is nothing better than peace, and Christmastime is a time for peace, however, what about the other eleven months of the year? For the past several years, I have made December my month to reflect, look back, and make amends with people I have hurt or who have hurt me, giving me the chance to begin the new year fresh and clean. Then I began to practice this throughout the year, and it has made all the difference in my life.

The angels said, "Glory to God." God gets glory when we are at peace and extend goodwill to all. As one committed to living a life beyond ordinary, let this be your season of peace and goodwill. Extend forgiveness and mercy to the Judas in your life, today.

Use your smartphone or tablet QR code reader to watch an important video about beyond ordinary living! Or, enter this link in your web browser: www.livingbeyondordinary.org/videos/chapter3.

Tweet these!

What is your greatest enemy to living beyond ordinary? #enemies http://bit.ly/1pVu3o1

What force is holding you back from living beyond ordinary? #breakingfree http://bit.ly/1pVu3o1

"Our human compassion binds us the one to the other—not in pity or patronizingly, but as human beings who have learnt how to turn our common suffering into hope for the future."—Nelson Mandela

~

"The purpose of human life is to serve, and to show compassion and the will to help others."—Albert Schweitzer

~

"God's dream is that you and I and all of us will realize that we are family; that we are made for togetherness, for goodness, and for compassion."—Desmond Tutu

~

"Compassion is the basis of morality."—Arthur Schopenhauer

~

"You may call God love, you may call God goodness. But the best name for God is compassion."—Meister Eckhart

~

"Things don't just happen in this world of arising and passing away. We don't live in some kind of crazy, accidental universe. Things happen according to certain laws, laws of nature, laws such as the law of karma, which teaches us that as a certain seed gets planted, so will that fruit be."—Sharon Salzberg

~

CHAPTER 4

THE BEYOND ORDINARY HEART

"Pastor Scott, I'm sorry to have to tell you this, but we are out of food and we're turning people away." Helping families with food assistance is a very big component of what we do, and for a local charity, we handle an extremely large volume (yes, helping 300-400 families a day requires *a lot* of food). In fact, each day, several large "eighteen-wheelers" pull in and drop off food for our campus. So in short, hearing this report from one of our staff members was not a great way to start the week.

Knowing that so many people count on us is all the motivation our loving staff needs to do the hard work they do, day in and day out. They work tirelessly to find the food and make sure it arrives, is unloaded, and made available on a daily basis. So when the team member gave me the terrible news, she did so with a tear in her eye. All she and I could see in our minds was the desperate moms and dads, unable to feed their families, senior citizens without nutritious fruits and vegetables, and working poor parents unable to provide for their teenagers.

The food supply is very seasonal; one month there is abundance, and the next month food can be hard to find. We try to maintain a constant supply, but many times this is totally out of our control and we are dependent on the law of supply and demand. This particular season was very low and we were really struggling to locate and purchase food in the secondary market. Although we receive a lot of food through donations from churches or corporations, it is never nearly enough. The pressure to find food can be overwhelming under normal circumstances, but during this season I could see the strain on the faces of our staff members.

I called the staff together to compare notes on everyone's efforts. They were all making the right calls, doing everything we all knew to do—it just wasn't working. I could see that fear and frustration had begun to set in. Though we had worked very hard and prayed very hard, our efforts just weren't good enough.

We needed a miracle.

Inside, I was panicking big time, but I knew that what my team needed from me was confidence and assurance, so that is what they saw. With words of full of faith and encouragement, I cheered the team on. We prayed once again and then dismissed. I made a point of walking back to my office by way of the grocery center so I could see the faces of the children, single moms and dads, and senior citizens—by the hundreds. They were lingering there just in case a truck full of food did arrive. I walked very slowly to see as many faces as I could. I wanted their faces imprinted on my heart. I wanted it to burn in me that these people were counting on us for help . . . and hope.

I made it back to my office, shut the door, and prayed a simple prayer: "God, this is not my problem—this is way too big a problem for us to handle. We need you. Please help us so we can help all these people who are counting on us." It wasn't a long or polished prayer, but it was sincere.

The Empty Warehouse

A few days passed and nothing seemed to have changed; still, no food. Every day that passed with no new deliveries meant we were in very big trouble. I wasn't surprised when key staff members pulled me aside and asked me to meet them in the warehouse. I knew what was coming and tried to avoid it, but I had to lead with confidence, both in good times and in times of crisis, so I met with them. They showed me the back warehouse, which was normally packed to the ceiling with food, ready to be placed on shelves. The message was loud and clear: "This is why we are very concerned." When I saw the empty warehouse, I too shared in their fear and concern. I had never seen the warehouse so empty—not since opening day. Food had always been available, every day since then. Though shaken, I remained outwardly calm and optimistic.

Our normally upbeat staff had met their match. They were fatigued and frustrated. They asked question after question and wanted answers. I was equally perplexed, unsure of what to say and unable to satisfy their questions or offer much needed direction. They weren't beating me up, but they definitely wanted answers and direction. By this time, the entire board of directors was in a panic as well and thought it best to make our supporters and donors aware of our dilemma. We were all concerned, but no one had the silver bullet we needed to solve the problem we faced.

Time for a Miracle

The only thing I knew to do was lean on the only answer I had: prayer to God. I gathered the staff together once again and prayed a brief, heartfelt prayer. After dismissing the meeting, everyone went back to their responsibilities. I went back to my office, shut the door, and stared at the ceiling for a few minutes. Then I booted up my computer to answer a few emails and get my mind off the problem.

Fifteen minutes into my busywork, there was great commotion outside my office. I tried to focus, but it became too distracting, so I went to see what was going on. With each step I took, it was clear the noise was coming from the warehouse. I quickened my pace.

I entered the warehouse and saw the answer to our prayers—nineteen answers, to be exact. In what had been an empty warehouse less than twenty minutes before, there were now nineteen pallets of food!

By the time I arrived, word had spread and the entire staff was running to the warehouse to see what was happening. We were swept up in the joy, as tears, laughter, relief, and amazement flowed. The warehouse team was so giddy; I could hardly get them to stop long enough to tell me what had happened. It turns out, almost immediately after our desperate prayer there had been a series of loud knocks at the back door to the loading area. Our warehouse manager opened the door to find a truck driver who had backed up his truck to our loading area. "Could you guys use some food?" he asked. "Absolutely!" our manager said. Then he watched in amazement, as nineteen pallets of food were unloaded into our warehouse.

"This God stuff is really getting to me!"

As we celebrated this special delivery, I remember one of our staff members coming up to me, patting me on the back, and saying: "This is unbelievable! This God stuff is really getting to me." It was getting to me, too! I was flabbergasted at what we had just experienced. It was by far one of the greatest miracles I had ever experienced. This lifted my faith. It also gave staff morale a much-needed boost. Most importantly, the senior citizens, single moms and dads, and other families would get the food they needed. From that moment on, we enjoyed an abundance of food for many years. Our warehouse never experienced emptiness like that ever again. Every once in a while, I see a truck backed up to our loading dock and it reminds me of that day when a truck driver showed up unexpectedly and asked a local food bank in downtown Orlando if they could use some food.

Hopefully, by now you're starting to get the idea of how big our operation is. It is not a mere church food pantry, but more like a Costco or Sam's Club warehouse: forklifts, tractor-trailers, and all. More than food, we provide those in need with a medical clinic, a crisis center, job training programs, a thrift center, and so much more. Every day is an absolute blast, but an awful lot of activity and work—and I mean work! We accomplish this due to the Christlike hearts of our loving, committed staff, and an army of volunteers.

Those who would live beyond ordinary lives have learned several keys that help them stay focused and on target to accomplish great things, even in difficult times. They surround themselves with people who are loving, committed, and hardworking, who encourage them and lift them up. They understand the importance and value of loving people. They learn from their mistakes and rise above their past. Finally, they do everything in their power to overcome any and all obstacles to accomplish their calling and mission.

"Those who would live beyond ordinary lives have learned several keys that help them stay focused and on target to accomplish great things, even in difficult times."

People of the Year

TIME magazine's Person of the Year award is, according to their website, "bestowed by the editors on the person or persons who most affected the news and our lives, for good or ill, and embodied what was important about the year." A few years ago, *TIME* magazine named three people as recipients of this award who, at first glance (to me), seemed like unlikely candidates for the honor: Bill and Melinda Gates, and Bono. Bill Gates is the billionaire founder of Microsoft, the world's largest software company, and Bono is the lead singer of the world famous rock group, U2. I was intrigued by the caption beneath the picture of them on the cover of *TIME*: "The Good Samaritans." My thoughts were: *How inappropriate to name these secular icons as Good Samaritans. Good Samaritan titles should be reserved for popes, clergy, or others doing great works of service and compassion.* I was surprised they had been chosen, that is, until I heard them express their hearts of love and compassion, and learned more about their charitable work.

As I read the article and heard the passion of all three of their hearts, I quickly came to the conclusion that I had been remarkably ignorant about the three of them. Qualities of the Good Samaritan character in the Bible parable jumped out at me as I read the *TIME* article. I noted that beyond their words, their actions and works reflected their true hearts, and my perspective changed. Those living beyond ordinary lives possess qualities of the Good Samaritan. Their actions and works speak volumes about what it means to genuinely love others, and to live lives of significance.

The Parable of the Good Samaritan

On one occasion an expert in the law stood up to test Jesus. "Teacher," he asked, "what must I do to inherit eternal life?"

"What is written in the Law?" he replied. "How do you read it?"

He answered, "'Love the Lord your God with all your heart and with all your soul and with all your strength and with all your mind' ; and, 'Love your neighbor as yourself.'"

"You have answered correctly," Jesus replied. "Do this and you will live."

But he wanted to justify himself, so he asked Jesus, "And who is my neighbor?"

In reply Jesus said: "A man was going down from Jerusalem to Jericho, when he was attacked by robbers. They

stripped him of his clothes, beat him and went away, leaving him half dead. A priest happened to be going down the same road, and when he saw the man, he passed by on the other side. So too, a Levite, when he came to the place and saw him, passed by on the other side. But a Samaritan, as he traveled, came where the man was; and when he saw him, he took pity on him. He went to him and bandaged his wounds, pouring on oil and wine. Then he put the man on his own donkey, brought him to an inn and took care of him. The next day he took out two denarii and gave them to the innkeeper. 'Look after him,' he said, 'and when I return, I will reimburse you for any extra expense you may have.'
"Which of these three do you think was a neighbor to the man who fell into the hands of robbers?"
The expert in the law replied, "The one who had mercy on him." Jesus told him, "Go and do likewise." (Luke 10:25-37, NIV)

In that day, the infamous road between Jerusalem and Jericho was particularly dangerous. It wasn't large or wide, so it was a perfect place for robbers and criminals to hide and ambush wealthy businessmen who traveled from Jerusalem to Jericho. In fact, locals called the road "bloody pass" due to the terror and pain so many had experienced on it.

After a long day of business, a Jewish man was on his way from Jerusalem to Jericho. Violent thieves seized the opportunity and jumped the man, leaving him nearly dead. A religious leader saw the injured man, but then looked at his daily activity list and decided to pass him by. Then a Levite, an apprentice to the priest, saw the injured man and made the decision to pass him by, as did his mentor. Finally, the Samaritan, who by custom was not allowed to talk or interact with Jews, crossed over to the other side and helped the Jewish man who was so desperately in need.

Good Samaritan Lessons for Living Beyond Ordinary

1. Helping people in need is important to God.

Notice that Jesus tells us the story of the Good Samaritan in response to a question from a lawyer, "How do we get to heaven?" Jesus answered the question by telling this iconic parable. In short, the best way to make sure you get to heaven, is to care for those in need. Our faith is best lived out in the love we express to those in need. Of course, we don't get to heaven solely on the merit of our works. However, because we are headed to heaven, we do good works. You've heard it said, "Faith without works is dead." Putting feet to our faith is important to God, so it ought to be important to us as well, as we live beyond ordinary lives (#LivingBeyondOrdinary).

2. No religious activity should ever be more important than helping people.

The priest and Levite in the parable had religious responsibilities to attend to at the temple. However, whatever the job was that they needed to do; it should not have taken priority over helping a man in immediate danger and need. God was not asking these religious leaders to neglect their job at the temple, but to actually do it: Help the man in need, lying right in front of you.

"God was not asking these religious leaders to neglect their job at the temple, but to actually do it: Help the man in need, lying right in front of you."

The priest and Levite not only had their priorities out of order, they had forgotten that nothing was more important than helping people. They had passed up "true religion" for a counterfeit. Of them, Dr. Martin Luther King, Jr., writes: "The first question which the priest and the Levite asked was: 'If I stop to help this man, what will happen to me?' But . . . the Good Samaritan reversed the question: 'If I do not stop to help this man, what will happen to me?'" Those who would live beyond ordinary lives embrace true religion and make helping people job #1.

3. At times, religious people can be hard-hearted when responding to the needs of those who are struggling.

If any group of people should be sensitive to the cry of the poor, it should be those who practice religion. Sadly, my experience has proven over and over that I cannot make this assumption. There are many very religious people who display huge hearts toward the needs of the poor, however, I have also seen many people others describe as "very spiritual people," who display nothing close to the compassion and passion I would expect. Those who would live beyond ordinary lives have big hearts for the poor and needy.

4. The Good Samaritan crossed the road: He was "all in."

The parable specifically says that the Good Samaritan "crossed over to the other side." When he made the decision to cross over, he was "all in." He committed himself to see his act of compassion and kindness through to the end, no matter the time, money, or effort it would require. Those who would live beyond ordinary lives are "all in" kind of people.

5. The Good Samaritan worked with others to get the job done.

The Samaritan knew that though he wasn't responsible to do everything, he had to do something. He was smart enough to know that there were others who could step up and help in the process, and did not fall into the guilt of the "I have to do it all" mentality. He networked and partnered with others to see the Jewish man restored to health and wellness. Those who would live beyond ordinary lives do their part to meet the needs of others.

6. The Good Samaritan knew it takes money to help people in need.

The beyond ordinary person realizes that it takes funds to help those in need. Money is not evil; the love of money is evil. It takes a tremendous amount of money to truly help people in poverty. Money does not solve all problems, but it is a key ingredient for doing so, along with kindness and compassion.

7. The Good Samaritan understood that where he spent his time revealed where his love and priorities lay.

If I were to spend a few days with you and shadow you, it is likely I would quickly find out how you spend your time, and thus, where your heart and priorities are. If we defer our expressions of care and compassion to a fraction of our time, and typically pass by people in need, we cannot say—with integrity—that we are truly walking in love as Christ did, or that hurting people are a priority in our lives. Those who would live beyond ordinary lives make it a priority to see the needs of others and meet them with love and compassion (#goodsamaritan).

"Those who would live beyond ordinary lives make it a priority to see the needs of others and meet them with love and compassion (#goodsamaritan)."

---

8. Good Samaritans do what others are unwilling to do.

It's one thing to see a man sitting on the side of a road with a sign, "Will work for food." It's totally another thing to stop what you are doing and do something about his hunger. It is one thing to hear of schoolchildren who have no money for even a basic lunch. When we do something about it, we live out Christ's life and love on this earth. When we make even just a little effort to do something about the needs we see, we experience fulfillment and joy and begin to live out our faith with works, moving closer to living a beyond ordinary life (#goodtogreat).

A few years ago, my youngest daughter, Allison, would always wake up and make her lunch for school. For a few weeks, I noticed she was making two sandwiches and two bags of lunch. The first few days, I thought it might be that she was growing and her appetite was getting bigger. Finally, one day I asked her about the amount of food she was taking to school each day. She calmly and confidently explained to me that a friend of hers from school showed up hungry every day. She was from a single parent home and had no food at home to bring to school, and no money for lunch. I loved the fact that my daughter did so much more than simply see her friend's need, but took it upon herself to do something about it. Allison's passion for meeting her friend's need continually serves as a reminder to me to do what others are unwilling to do.

9. Good Samaritans feel what others do not feel.

Emotions are a big part of life. Imagine going to a college football game and, as you enter the stadium, the person taking your ticket informs you that you must show no emotion during the game. That rule would be broken immediately! Why? A football game without emotion is boring, unrealistic, and no fun. What's a football game without shouting, screaming, while painted up with your team's colors? Similarly, living life without allowing our hearts to feel what those who are hurting are feeling can leave us hard-hearted and feeling flat, emotionally. This is why our world is filled with unemotional, hard-hearted people who choose to live unsympathetic and even mean-spirited lives: They refuse to feel what others are going through.

Make the choice today to live beyond ordinary and feel the sorrow of a friend who has lost a child, the devastation of the coworker who has lost her home, or the desperation of the single mom who is struggling to make ends meet. Feel what they are feeling, reach out to God in faith, and in every way possible, help them experience God's peace and love.

10. *Good Samaritans touch what others refuse to touch.*

I remember when the AIDS epidemic first swept our nation with ferocious force, and hundreds of thousands of people died over the course of just a few years. One of the many misconceptions common at the time was that even casual contact with someone with AIDS—even the slightest touch—could make you vulnerable to contracting the virus. This misinformation caused many in our nation to avoid those suffering from this illness, at all costs. This was not just a shame, but incredibly devastating to those who were suffering, who could have received so much emotionally from some loving human contact.

I have seen the power of a simple touch—the power of even simply holding the hand of one who is suffering. I have seen strength transfer from one person to another through a hug. Love and encouragement transfer when someone with a compassionate hand merely touches a person in need, offers a simple pat on the back, or shares an honest tear with another in pain. Touch offers hope, encouragement, and acceptance.

Go ahead; reach out and touch someone today. It may be the very thing a hurting person needs to get back on track. Those who would live beyond ordinary lives understand the power of touch to express love, compassion, and encouragement.

11. *Good Samaritans hear what others do not hear.*

Many times, we are all so busy that we don't really hear what is happening around us. Every day, our family members, neighbors, coworkers, and friends give us clues about tough times they are going through, and we hear them . . . but really don't listen. If you and I make the continuous decision to hear others' cries of hurt, pain, and struggle, it will transform our hearts, filling them with love, compassion, and wisdom. Those who live beyond ordinary lives hear what others do not or will not hear.

Lessons from a Good Samaritan Truck Driver

A truck driver I had never met, driving a truck from who knows where, dropped off nineteen pallets of food in answer to our simple prayer. I'll probably never get to meet that driver, but I'll certainly never forget what he did and what it meant to all of us. To me, typical of a Good Samaritan, he probably doesn't even know the impact he made on me and thousands of people in Central Florida. The beauty of living beyond ordinary is that, many times, you don't really ever know the impact you are making. To you, you are just living your life, when actually, your life is distributing hope, healing, and help you're unaware of, most of the time. No matter who you are, you can change and impact others' lives just by naturally living out the beyond ordinary heart with purpose and significance, consumed with God's love and compassion.

There will be a special place in heaven for people who see what others don't see, do what others won't do, feel what others don't feel, and touch what others won't touch. That truck driver, the members of our staff, and the Good Samaritan—these are the real heroes who inspire me to continue to live life outside my comfort zone . . . beyond ordinary.

Use your smartphone or tablet QR code reader to watch an important video about beyond ordinary living! Or, enter this link in your web browser: www.livingbeyondordinary.org/videos/chapter4.

Tweet these!

What can you do to become a Good Samaritan? #goodsamaritan
http://bit.ly/1pVu3o1

How do you move from good to great Samaritan? #goodtogreat
http://bit.ly/1pVu3o1

"Once you replace negative thoughts with positive ones, you'll start having positive results."—Willie Nelson

~

"Positive anything is better than negative nothing."
—Elbert Hubbard

~

"Positive thinking will let you do everything better than negative thinking will."—Zig Ziglar

~

"It takes but one positive thought when given a chance to survive and thrive to overpower an entire army of negative thoughts."
—Robert H. Schuller

~

"I've always believed that you can think positive just as well as you can think negative."—James A. Baldwin

~

"Think twice before you speak, because your words and influence will plant the seed of either success or failure in the mind of another."—Napoleon Hill

~

CHAPTER 5

BEYOND ORDINARY THINKING

The Rodriguez family was living the American dream: a great marriage, fun-filled home life, good paying jobs, and healthy children. Their world came crashing down when the doctors informed them that the youngest Rodriguez son, Jose, had a life-threatening illness. The doctors in the Rodriguez' hometown of Columbus, Ohio, didn't have many options for them, other than to tell them to get to Orlando to see if Arnold Palmer Hospital could possibly help them. So, they packed up all their belongings, uprooted their entire family, and headed to Orlando, Florida, for what they hoped would be a life-changing adventure that would culminate in their son finding healing. They sacrificially left all they knew behind—their home, family, friends, and jobs—to see that Jose received the care he needed to survive.

Upon arrival, distant relatives offered them a place to stay, but after only a few days the arrangement proved to be too much for both families, and the offer was retracted. The Rodriguez family found itself homeless and out of options. The hospital provided wonderful care and treatment for Jose, but couldn't offer the family much help in meeting their long-term housing and employment needs.

One day, the hospital social worker met with Jenny Rodriguez to help with their crisis. She had a long list of Central Florida non-profits and charities in her folder that could potentially offer the Rodriquez family some relief. "Here's a list of places that might be able to help you," she said as she handed the list to Jenny. Then she walked Jenny to a window and pointed in the direction of our Community Food and Outreach Center (CFOC), as our campus is just a few miles south of the hospital. "However, if I were you, I would go to that place on Michigan Street. You'll get help there."

Jenny and Markus Rodriguez showed up at CFOC and, after a few weeks of phone calls, meetings, and clinical assessments, our caring staff was able to secure long-term housing, jobs for both of them, an automobile (donated by a local car dealer), and saw that the Rodriguez children were placed in public schools. Most importantly, they made it possible for Jose to receive the treatment he needed to gain a new lease on life.

In a note to one of our counselors, Jenny would later recount:

> My mind was racing all the time with hopeless thoughts of desperation. I couldn't avoid the loud screams of fear that seemed to follow me—and at times—torment me.
>
> I found peace with my situation when I would simply slow down and be quiet in the midst of my storm, think about God, and put my trust in Him.
>
> When I was at my weakest points and totally discouraged, it seemed like my closest friends would be there for me and lift me with positive words of encouragement, lifting my spirit and giving me the inner strength to fight on.
>
> My faith gave me the courage to fight through the difficult and lonely days. If not for the wonderful

promises and hope-filled words from the Bible and my friends, I'm not sure I could have made it through this devastating season.

Jenny never gave up! In her darkest moments, she thrived on the encouragement, promises, and hope-filled words of dear friends, and her Bible. She trusted God and believed things would turn around for her and her family. Life-threatening illness was an intimidating foe, and uprooting her entire family was life altering, but Jenny's ability to think positively and stand in faith empowered her to make it through her "devastating season." Jenny's thoughts and beliefs led her to live a beyond ordinary life (#LivingBeyondOrdinary).

Thanksgiving Without Turkey

Several years ago, we were in the middle of our annual Thanksgiving outreach to our community. Our goal was to collect and distribute 2,000 care boxes that would each feed an average of 4-6 family members. Each care box would contain all the canned and packaged goods for a traditional Thanksgiving meal, along with a $10-$15 gift certificate for a turkey. Our budget for this outreach is typically between $25,000 and $30,000 per year, above our normal monthly operational expenses. Though this brings additional pressure each year, it is certainly worth it.

A massive undertaking, our Thanksgiving outreach involves hundreds of volunteers and many large rental trucks that run regular routes, collecting donated food items from all over our area, including those from over thirty public and private schools. We begin planning and logistics in the spring and summer just to get ready for it. It's all worth it, being able to provide a little relief for children and families in need during this very special holiday. Every year, this fantastic week of blessing is a smashing success. Churches, corporations, neighbors, and countless others get great joy from making it happen.

By far, Thanksgiving is the best time of year for me. It allows me the privilege of sitting down with my family at Thanksgiving to recall all that we are thankful for, and fills my heart with joy and a deep sense of accomplishment, knowing that literally thousands of families are enjoying the same meal all over Central Florida.

This time, as always, at the beginning of the campaign, I was full of faith and belief that we would pull off the Thanksgiving outreach successfully once again. I had confidence in our staff, board, volunteers, and community; that it would all come together. I believe that God is never early, but He's always on time, and have found this to be true, time and again. In projects big and small, it always seems to be true, and I believed this year would be no exception.

Everything was clicking along perfectly and according to plan. Everyone seemed happy and positive, and the schools, churches, and corporations were collecting more food than ever before. We had plenty of motivated volunteers, excitement was building, and hopes were high.

Then one day, a few staff members came to me, concerned that though we had plenty of canned and packaged foods to fill each box, financial donations to purchase gift certificates for turkeys were way behind. At first, I was not concerned. However, when those same staff members pulled me aside mere hours before the deadline, I was greatly concerned. "We are 700 short on turkey gift certificates for the care boxes," they said. I quickly calculated we had a $7,000 problem and nearly zero time to solve it. If we didn't, several thousand children, teenagers, adults, and senior citizens would have Thanksgiving without turkey. To me, this was a "zero tolerance issue": Thanksgiving is not Thanksgiving without turkey. We had one day to find $7,000.

After years of doing this type of work, I have developed a very strong faith to believe for the impossible. After seeing the impossible happen time and time again, it tends to build one's faith and confidence. Our team had also seen the impossible happen time and again. So faith and belief were deep in our DNA. Over the years, we had learned to trust in God and knew that He would provide. We did not accept failure or defeat.

It was a long drive home that night. The sleepless night that followed was even worse. Some may think it's wrong to deal with your emotions when you are in the midst of a life battle. A life battle is just that—it's a fight, a struggle. It's fine to struggle and wrestle with your faith, emotions, and fears from time to time. Every great beyond ordinary leader has and will have times when, in spite of believing in what they are doing, they still have inward turmoil. This internal battle is not a sign of weakness or doubt, but a reflection of their humanity. It's perfectly normal and acceptable to have moments of uncertainty.

Deadline Day

It was the morning of deadline day. I'll never forget it. In spite of conversations with God, our staff, our board members, and Tammi, I approached the day physically exhausted, mentally drained, and emotionally spent. We were running out of time: A decision had to be made. The battle for my mind raged as discouragement warred against my positive thoughts and attitude that had worked to create an atmosphere of expectation.

When I arrived at our rented warehouse, I knew I had to remain upbeat and positive as I approached the staff and hundreds of volunteers. As the morning passed, I walked around thanking volunteers, took photos, stacked a few boxes, and tried to keep busy so I wouldn't let my mind think about the dilemma we faced.

Just then, I noticed a man approach the door and stand next to our sign-in table for volunteers. I assumed he was there to volunteer, so I greeted him and handed him the volunteer form to fill out. He quickly and politely told me he was not there to volunteer, but just wanted to see what we were doing. He was genuinely interested in what we were up to and asked me many questions. I was glad to answer. Finally, he asked about our goal and if we were going to meet it. Without crying or poor mouthing, I simply told him the truth: We were a little short, but believed the additional funds would come in so we could meet our goal of feeding hundreds of children and families. We talked for a few more minutes, but then an issue arose and I had to get back to work. He said good-bye and wished us luck.

The $7,000 Miracle

I completely forgot about the conversation I had with the man and dove into the final work that needed to be completed. I didn't give it another thought until he walked back into the warehouse a few hours later. When I saw him, I recognized him immediately. Hot, sweaty, and in need of a break, I stepped away from the work and greeted him again. The gentleman (I never asked him his name) asked me to come back to the sign-up table.

"I like what you are doing and want to help you," he said.

I responded with a hearty, "Great!" as I wiped the sweat from my forehead. "What would you like to do? Would you like to stack boxes? Drive a truck? Assemble care boxes?"

"No," he said, "I want to help with the turkeys."

"Wow, that's wonderful. Thank you very much," I said enthusiastically.

Then he did something I will never forget—something no one has done before or since. He proceeded to place in my hand seventy $100 bills. I stood there in stunned silence for a moment. After I thanked him, I thought I might faint. I was in shock. He patted me on the back and said: "God bless you. Go get your turkeys. Happy Thanksgiving!" Then he walked out, never to be seen by us again, unfortunately. Seconds later, I ran out to the local supermarket and purchased 700 gift certificates for turkeys. Ever since then, every Thanksgiving, I remember that man's face and thank God for what he did for thousands of children and families that miraculous day.

Once again, we had seen the impossible happen.

The Giant Who Killed Goliath

There is a well-known story found in the Old Testament about a young man named David, and a giant, Goliath. If you are like me, you've heard the account of their battle a million times. It's an incredible story—one that motivates me to face and confront big obstacles with faith and courage. However, I like to look at the story a little differently. I look at David as a giant much bigger than Goliath—not physically of course, but mentally and spiritually. David believed he would defeat the giant. He had only faith that his God would empower him to win the battle. He stood in expectation of victory (#giantkillers). His attitude and thought life inspired him to face challenges on all levels, and to fight with boldness and tenacity:

> "I can do this."

> "I've seen God's faithfulness before; His faithfulness is great."

> "Goliath is not really a giant to me. I'm the giant, in God, and my faith is big."

> "This is not impossible."

> "When I am afraid, I will trust in you, Lord."

David was a strong young man in body, but I believe he was much stronger in his faith and mind. Goliath was an intimidating force. He made a career out of intimidating and humiliating enemies and opponents. He used words to strike fear, insecurity, and humiliation in the hearts of his enemies. In fact, many of the soldiers in the Israeli army were so overwhelmed by Goliath's intimidation that, according to 1 Samuel 18, they literally ran away in fear for their lives. That had to be quite an unforgettable image for a young man to see: mature men running for their lives at the mere trash talk of an intimidating adversary. To then face that same adversary shows David's incredible level of faith and courage.

"David believed he would defeat the giant. He had only faith that his God would empower him to win the battle. He stood in expectation of victory (#giantkillers)."

David had developed an attitude and thought life that Goliath's words could not influence or overcome. In the face of fear, David was fearless. Beyond ordinary people do not cower to the negative words, thoughts, or attitudes that are thrown at them. Beyond ordinary people thrive when the battle rages. They are giants who live and walk by faith (#iamagiant).

Becoming a Giant, Like David

1. Giants are strong in mind and spirit.

The battle between David and Goliath was not necessarily a physical battle; it was all about the mind. Goliath's method of operation was to intimidate and cause people to fear him due to his size. Physically, David was outmatched; but this had nothing to do with body size. It had everything to do with the size of the spirit, and David was the giant because he was strong in his trust and thought life.

2. Giants use beyond ordinary weapons to defeat their enemy.

Five stones were not an ordinary weapon for most people of David's time. I believe David's five stones meant something to him. I like to think each one represented a past victory of his. David knew he could fight armed with five little stones because he believed they possessed power.

"Beyond ordinary people thrive when the battle rages. They are giants who live and walk by faith (#iamagiant)."

When the enemy tries to intimidate you with negative, fearful thoughts and lies, think of these as five smooth stones in your sling and use them to battle him:

~ God loves me.

~ God has a plan for me.

~ God believes in me.

~ God gives me the courage I need to fight.

~ God gives victory in life.

3. Giants run to the battle line, not from it.

Goliath wasn't going anywhere. David knew this and ran forward with confidence and courage to battle Goliath. Similarly, your problems are not magically going away. The Goliaths in your life will continue to taunt you and scream their discouragement as long as you allow them to. Once you begin to run toward the battle, each step you take will fill you with faith and courage.

4. Giants are not intimidated by humiliating words.

Goliath's words were empty threats. David chose not to allow these negative words to discourage him or distract him. Positive thoughts and words of faith, hope, and belief filled his heart and mind, leaving no room for the enemy to gain power over him.

5. Giants live by supernatural faith, not by natural sight.

If David had looked at his situation through his natural eyes, he might have given up. David saw his all-powerful God as far bigger than Goliath. Just as God had delivered the lion and the bear into his hands, David had faith that God would deliver Goliath into his hands. His eyes were fixed on God, not Goliath.

6. Giants inspire others to fight and win.

The war-hardened veteran soldiers of the Israeli army were inspired by David's faith. Soldiers who had run for their lives just a few hours earlier were inspired by young David's faith and courage. They found new heights of faith and depths of courage to face their giants.

We are called to inspire one another. As the head of our outreach, I understand how important it is for our team to see me walking in faith and courage, even in the face of the most intimidating adversity. This inspires them to find new heights of faith and depths of courage for facing their giants.

I have found it very helpful to memorize and quote verses or short passages of Scripture that inspire me and motivate me. This helps to fortify my heart for when I face stressful times, and am attacked by that poisonous voice that screams venomous lies to incite fear, doubt, and discouragement in my heart. This voice is not audible, but it is memorable and distinct:

> "You're going to fail!"
>
> "You have finally reached a wall—you can go no further."
>
> "What will people think?"
>
> "You cannot recover from this."

Bible verses and passages may seem smaller and calmer, but they are so much stronger. They don't try to compete with voices of doubt and fear because the voice of faith is confident in itself and its power, so it speaks very quietly, yet reassuringly.

One of the reasons I try to maintain a positive attitude and keep my thoughts moving in an upward direction is because I know that many people are counting on me and our team. One wrong attitude or thought on my part could poison the attitudes and thoughts of many others, potentially disrupting services and affecting hundreds, if not thousands, of children and families.

"... don't try to compete with voices of doubt and fear because the voice of faith is confident in itself and its power, so it speaks very quietly, yet reassuringly."

This is why I am very careful to pay attention to which voice I am listening to—the voice of fear or the voice of faith. I also try very hard to surround myself with people who are filled with words of courage and wisdom. In stressful times especially, I surround myself with staff members, friends, and family who believe in the power of words and the power of positive thoughts.

Over the years, I have held onto one particular verse that continually inspires and motivates me: "Because of the Lord's great love we are not consumed, for his compassions never fail. They are new every morning; great is your faithfulness" (Lamentations 3:22-23, NIV). "I say to myself, 'The Lord is my portion; therefore I will wait for him" (Lamentations 3:24, NIV). I'm so glad this passage doesn't say that His faithfulness is average or good. They say, "GREAT is your faithfulness." Every day, we can face huge mountains that will try to intimidate us and cause us to run away in fear, but we can trust Him and rely on His faithfulness.

A few years ago, my second son, Aaren, was playing high school baseball for his Christian school. He was a great athlete (just like his old man) and certainly had the skill and ability, but he was struggling mentally—frustration and doubt were written all over his face. Day after day, he tried to fight through it, but he only seemed to fall deeper and deeper into a slump. His frustration was greatest every time he got up to the plate and faced the pitcher. You could see the fear grip him whenever he caught the ball or threw it to the infielders. Routine plays became impossible for him. Finally, after allowing him to try fighting through it for a few weeks, I stepped up. I didn't give a sermon or lecture; I just asked for his baseball cap. As he fell asleep that night, anxious for the next day's game, I said a prayer for him. Then I used a Sharpie pen to write a simple, strong, steadfast verse on the inside brim of his cap: "When I am afraid, I put my trust in you" (Psalm 56:3, NIV). Over the years, this verse had helped me tremendously when I faced various fears. My strategy was simple: If it worked for me, it would work for him.

The next morning, as he got ready for school, I handed his cap to him and told him I'd be praying for him . . . and that I believed in him. Then as he left, I casually said with a smile, "I left a note for you, inside the brim of your hat. Take a look at it during the game; I think it will help you."

I would love to say that Aaren miraculously hit a grand slam that afternoon. He didn't. I think he went 0-4, with two errors, but I noticed the power of his positive thoughts and meditation that day. Though nothing seemed to change on the outside, inwardly, the words were making an impact. Like small seeds dropped in the ground, those words of love, acceptance, and courage would sprout up soon. (As his dad, I was hoping they would spring up just in time for the playoffs!)

Boy, was my timing great! In a few games, his stroke was back, his confidence was on track, and his swing was smooth. Aaren had walked through a life lesson of listening to that still small voice and silencing the voice of fear, doubt, and discouragement. He learned the same lesson Jenny Rodriguez learned during her "devastating season." We all need to fill up on positive thoughts, Bible verses, and encouragement to counter the hopeless, negative words that come against us. When we listen to words that inspire and motivate us, we end up on the winning side of life. Aaren's baseball cap is still up in his closet as a reminder that when things get tough, to simply look up, stand on a promise, and swing.

Use your smartphone or tablet QR code reader to watch an important video about beyond ordinary living! Or, enter this link in your web browser: www.livingbeyondordinary.org/videos/chapter5.

Tweet these!

What giants are you facing in your life? #giantkillers http://bit.ly/1pVu3o1

Do you see your obstacles as giant, or do you see yourself as a giant? #iamagiant http://bit.ly/1pVu3o1

"If you hear a voice within you say 'You cannot paint,' then by all means paint, and that voice will be silenced."—Vincent Van Gogh

~

"Anxiety in a man's heart weighs it down, but a good word makes it glad."—Solomon (Proverbs 12:25, NASB)

~

"Words are singularly the most powerful force available to humanity. We can choose to use this force constructively with words of encouragement, or destructively using words of despair. Words have energy and power with the ability to help, to heal, to hinder, to hurt, to harm, to humiliate and to humble."—Yehuda Berg

~

"A word of encouragement from a teacher to a child can change a life. A word of encouragement from a spouse can save a marriage. A word of encouragement from a leader can inspire a person to reach her potential."—John C. Maxwell

~

"When you encourage others, you in the process are encouraged because you're making a commitment and difference in that person's life. Encouragement really does make a difference."
—Zig Ziglar

~

"If we're going to bring out the best in people, we, too, need to sow seeds of encouragement."—Joel Osteen

~

CHAPTER 6

BEYOND ORDINARY SPEAKING

Anna is a senior citizen of Russian descent, who lives within walking distance of our campus. She stands only four feet, five inches tall, but is strong in spirit. She has been coming to our campus for twelve years, not because she wants to, but because she has to. She receives around $650 a month from social security, but after spending $200 a month on medicine, she does not have enough for housing, food, or much else. There are millions just like her who struggle each month and make desperate choices between paying for medicine or buying food. She comes to us for food, but I also know she comes for hope as well.

Many times, when she walks on campus, pulling her cart behind her, Anna's shoulders are slumped in discouragement and her face is downcast. She seems very lonely. I love to see her brighten up when I greet her with a hug. "Anna," I whisper to her each time, "we're here for you. You know that, don't you? We want you to know that you can depend on us to always be here when you need us."

A recurring agenda item at our staff meetings is me reminding our staff that loving on the people we serve is job one; and we are to bring life to them with a listening ear and words of love, acceptance, hope, comfort, and encouragement. If we have to stop a task—no matter what it is—to love on someone, then so be it. Sometimes I ask them to specifically target certain ones, like Anna, for an extra helping of love. It's amazing to see the impact of our words on her: her whole countenance changes. She smiles and walks just a little taller. You can just see her breathing in the life and healing.

It would be very easy for Anna and others to get lost in a city of 2 million people, like Orlando. I'm so glad she can come to a place where everyone knows her name, loves on her, and lifts her spirits.

Not long ago, we held a huge annual fundraising event at one of the largest churches in Orlando. This church is one of our biggest donors and a key partner in fighting poverty in Central Florida, and bringing hope and help to struggling families. The place was packed with over 600 of our most compassionate and kindhearted donors and friends, who joined with us to celebrate all the lives that had been touched and helped. I invited a very special guest to sit right next to Tammi and me at the front table: Anna. I wanted her to see and get to know the friends who supported us so we could help her and so many others.

At the very end of this event each year, I usually close with a speech of thanks and appreciation. This time, I brought Anna up on stage and simply let the donors know the impact they were having on that wonderful lady. Anna had been blown away all evening by all the friendly hugs and greetings of the people there, and determinedly put to use what little English she knew to give a heartfelt thank you to them. It was the most beautiful part of the program. As I listened to her express her thanks, I thought to myself: *All the loving, life-giving words we have spoken over her are now coming back full circle, blessing me and so many others.* It was a humbling, inspiring moment.

The Dream of a One-Stop Shop: Walmart of the Nonprofit World

For years, even when we had only the food pantry in operation, my dream had been to build a campus of hope and help; a place where those in need could come and find loving, caring people they could trust—a place they could count on to receive food assistance, crisis care, counseling, domestic abuse help, substance abuse assistance, educational training, and medical service (known as a "holistic services" entity in nonprofit parlance). I had noticed that having nonprofit services spread all over town created a great hardship on those who most needed them. Some people would spend all day, every day walking or taking the bus to various charities, that is, if they didn't just give up due to exhaustion, fatigue, or frustration. Our model would serve as a one-stop shop, meeting a wide range of needs in one facility.

Our model of offering multiple services at one campus is actually quite innovative (and prompted some to call us the "Walmart of the nonprofit world"). Many people who are hurting financially and struggling are very skeptical. They have been so hurt, wounded, or abused that they find it hard to trust and believe for good things. We know we are accomplishing our mission, earning the trust of the needy, and bringing hope to the desperate poor when families we serve look at us and say, "This place is too good to be true!"

The Clinic Vision

It was 5,000 square feet of raw, empty warehouse space. It didn't look like much. Those with expert eyes would likely look at it and shake their heads in disgust. I looked at it and was gripped by a sense of promise and destiny. Week after week, I would walk past the space and say aloud, "This is our clinic." I'm glad no one else was around because they would have thought I was crazy.

In the beginning, I felt a bit crazy. One day, I asked my trusted right hand/executive director to come with me to the warehouse to dream and speak life to part where the clinic would be. We both felt funny doing this, but after we did, we noticed the momentum and atmosphere started to change. It felt good.

After a few weeks of this, we met with a key board member, and with a little faith (and a bit of trepidation), shared the vision for the clinic, hoping we would not get laughed out of the building. To our amazement, the board member caught on and started believing with us, even joining us in speaking the vision: "This is our clinic."

After a few more weeks, we met with the entire board and staff and suddenly, any hint of fear was gone. A spirit of faith filled the entire warehouse space as we all spoke words of life and purpose. Nothing had changed in the natural, but something unseen was happening. It didn't take long before we all knew the clinic was going to happen. Every day, we would simply speak what we believed. Boy, was it fun to watch and see the power of our words bring life to that space. It is remarkable, what can happen when people start speaking life, purpose, and destiny.

The Clinic Vision Realized

Many experts told us it couldn't be done, but we fought through the opposition and continued on our path, as time rolled on. Finally, in 2006, we connected with a few volunteer nurses and doctors, and started to open up our campus to offer medical help on Sunday mornings—the only morning our facility wasn't packed with people. It felt strange for me to miss Sunday morning church services, but I was reminded that what we were doing was "church outpoured," and by serving moms, dads, children, and senior citizens each Sunday, I was in the right place.

We were up and running, though our clinic was raw and simple—humble beginnings. At first, we set up a sign-in table and six examination rooms throughout the community center. Each was equipped with a six-foot white plastic folding table, covered with white clinical paper, and a few sheets hung around each one, for privacy. With volunteers set to maintain the records, greeters to meet those who needed medical attention, and a few nurse and doctors, we were on our way.

The first few months, our clinic was a bit sketchy, but our love and care were genuine. What we lacked in professionalism we made up for with passion. We treated every person who came in with dignity and respect, and offered them first class service.

The patients didn't care about the décor. They were grateful and appreciative to have access to medical care, as they had no other options. After a few months, people flocked to the clinic. Each Sunday, we served hundreds of people. We had struck a cord and were meeting a real need, but it quickly became clear that the Sunday clinic was simply not adequate to meet the need.

"What do you need me to do for you?"

We had a little money in the bank, but not nearly enough to get the clinic up and running beyond Sunday morning. We needed start-up funds. We didn't know how it would happen, but we knew it would happen. The clinic would be a reality.

One day, I received a call from an old Edgewater High School friend. He said he had heard about what we were doing and wanted to see it. Mother Teresa responded to people who wanted to see her medical hospital by saying, "Come and see." I'm no Mother Teresa, and our clinic is not a major hospital, but I believe in the concept of "come and see." (Any charity you can't go and see at any time of the day isn't worth supporting.) I responded to my high school buddy the same way Mother Teresa would have: "Come and see."

We met a few days later, and I could tell from the very beginning that this was going to be memorable. I didn't pressure or poor-mouth; I never do. I simply let him see, feel, and experience our mission. We walked outside and stood in the parking lot. I should mention, my friend is quite intimidating. He's six feet, four inches tall, has a dominant personality, and is hard to read, so I never expected to hear what he was about to say. "Scott," he said, "I have everything the world has to offer. I've been blessed." Then he teared up and said, "What do you need me to do for you?" Normally, when people say this, I play if off and tell them I'll get back to them (as sometimes people say this but really don't mean it). This time, however, I felt bold and courageous and quickly responded, "I need you to build me a clinic."

At first, I couldn't believe what I had said, but after I said it, it felt good, so I said it again. To my amazement, he said, "I'll do it." Boy, did he do it. One hundred and twenty days from that conversation, he mobilized volunteers, vendors, supporters, and contractors, and built a first-class professional medical clinic, with seven exam rooms and an office, fully furnished.

To this day, our clinic is up and running, helping hundreds and hundreds of children and families. It was our destiny to fulfill the dream of seeing this become a reality: a medical clinic was born.

A Beyond Ordinary Encounter

Now that the clinic was actually built . . . it seemed to be a good time to think about how to fund it. Sure, we had things a little backwards, but it seemed to work out. As miraculous as it was, getting the clinic built, the initial funding of the clinic was just as amazing.

One night, my wife, Tammi, was at dinner with several friends on Park Avenue in Winter Park, a beautiful area of parks, restaurants, and shopping. It was a girls' night out and they were all enjoying a nice evening together. At some point, one of her friends recognized a well-known, popular leader in the Central Florida area. The ladies approached the man's table and made small talk.

Somehow, the conversation turned to what Tammi and her husband did for a living. Since all the ladies at the table were donors and friends of the outreach, they enthusiastically talked about what we did for our community. They made quite an impression on the man with their genuine passion for what we did, because after the conversation, he simply handed Tammi his card and said: "Have Scott call me. I want to meet him."

Tammi came home that night and tossed the card on the table. "Here . . . he wants you to call him tomorrow." I get a lot of cards and people telling me to call them, so this was not uncommon. However, when I saw the name on *this* card, I almost fell out of my chair. The first words out of my mouth were, "You've got to be kidding." I couldn't believe what I was seeing. Then Tammi told me about her encounter with the man and all she and the other ladies had said and done. It was an incredible story.

It took me days, but I finally worked up the courage to give this man a call. I was surprised to have my call put right through to his office. I spoke with his assistant who confirmed that he did indeed want to see me. We scheduled a meeting for a few days later.

"You've got an hour. I want to hear your story."

Tammi and I made our way to downtown Orlando, to the man's office in a high-rise office building. After a few minutes in the lobby, we met with him. We were not scared or intimidated. We were confident in the mission we had started, but this was not an ordinary meeting, for sure; it was a big opportunity for us. After exchanging some small talk, he said: "You've got an hour. I want to hear your story." For the next hour, we shared our story. It went very well. I enjoyed the opportunity and was grateful, as always, to share the vision with others. At the close of our meeting, the man simply said, "I like what I hear. Give me a few days."

It doesn't matter how big or important people are; I share my passion with people with the same conviction, whether the hearer is rich or poor. I have always used this phrase as my motto: "If I go after the people no one wants, God will bring me the people everyone is after." This was certainly true in this case. As I remained faithful to the poor and needy, I believed that God would bring me before people who could help further the mission.

"I have always used this phrase as my motto: "If I go after the people no one wants, God will bring me the people everyone is after.""

A few days later, the man contacted me and asked that we prepare a proposal to fund the entire clinic with doctors, nurses, staff, and equipment. We complied and just a few months later, we received word that he had decided to fund the entire clinic. Those without access to medical care—children, teens, their parents, and the elderly—would now receive first-class medical treatment.

All this happened because two men on separate paths came together to unite with the spoken vision. One would build the clinic; the other would fund *all* the operational costs. They touched the heart of God together.

Voices of Faith

The Bible tells us a story of a paralyzed man that reinforces the need for us to speak words to one another that create life and destiny.

> A few days later, when Jesus again entered Capernaum, the people heard that he had come home. They gathered in such large numbers that there was no room left, not even outside the door, and he preached the word to them. Some men came, bringing to him a paralyzed man, carried by four of them. Since they could not get him to Jesus because of the crowd, they made an opening in the roof above

Jesus by digging through it and then lowered the mat the man was lying on. When Jesus saw their faith, he said to the paralyzed man, "Son, your sins are forgiven." (Mark 2:1-5, NIV)

Four Men, Four Voices

The crippled man knew he couldn't get to where he wanted to go by himself. He was smart enough to recruit four friends who would carry him to his miracle from Jesus (#beyondordinaryencounter). He didn't pick just anyone; he had a lot of time to think about the kind of people he wanted around him. He didn't want just anyone near him; he wanted men who would not only carry him physically, but who would carry his vision as well—his vision of getting well. He didn't want close friends who would discourage him and speak words of doubt and unbelief; he wanted words spoken near him that would lift him up and encourage him. I believe he picked four friends who were known to be full of faith, positive men, who spoke life (#beyondordinaryvoices).

The friends you pick to carry you will change, depending on the issue you are facing. If you are facing financial obstacles, you might pick friends who will speak words of wisdom and insight on practical matters. If you are facing troubles with relationships, you might pick friends who will speak words of wisdom and insight on matters of the heart. The point is, you must surround yourself with people who will speak words of encouragement, faith, hope, and courage (#LivingBeyondOrdinary).

Friend #1: Words of Encouragement

On your way to your miracle, you need someone in front of you. As they carry you, they speak words of encouragement. This person has to view the glass as half full, not half empty. They have to see forward and speak words to you that inspire you. Remember, you and I are like the crippled man. We can't see ahead. We can't move. We are paralyzed. We need a fighter in front who sees victory ahead.

Friend #2: Words of Faith

The second person who carries you on your way to your miracle is a voice of faith, not doubt. It's a long way to go, to truly see Jesus. There will be many obstacles and challenges. That's why you need a voice speaking words of faith to you, not doubt or despair. Find that person in your life that always inspires and motivates you to believe for the impossible. Surround yourself with people who will lift you up.

Friend #3: Words of Hope

The Bible says, "Hope deferred makes the heart sick" (Proverbs 13:12, NIV). As humans, we lose hope and get sick when we don't see any possibility of good on the horizon. This is why I encourage you to get a friend who will always speak hope and life. You'll need this person when you get depressed and discouraged. Their words of hope will cause you to soar and expect great things.

Friend #4: Words of Courage

We all need a voice speaking to us that inspires us to fight and not give up. The voice of courage provokes us to stay in the battle and keep fighting. Many times, we want to give up and quit, even though we are so very close to winning. The voice of courage gets us over the hump and moves us on to victory.

"The voice of courage provokes us to stay in the battle and keep fighting."

Of Faith and Football

A few years ago, my oldest son, Austen, was getting ready for a big playoff game for his high school football team. I could tell he was nervous about the game. At first, I really didn't know what to say. Knowing that words are powerful and have lasting impact, I waited and waited for the right voice to speak to me so I could speak words of peace and life to him.

I would love to say the words came in thirty seconds, but they didn't. I had to wait all night until I finally felt I had the right words to say. I waited for just the right moment, just before the ride to drop him off at school for the game, later that night. As calmly and coolly as a dad can before a big football game, I said: "Austen, I know you're nervous and stressed about the game tonight—it's a big game and a lot is riding on it." Then we arrived at the school parking lot. Knowing I only had a few seconds to make a dramatic point, as I put the car in park, with one hand on his shoulder, I said to him: "I want you to know that tonight, if you make every single tackle, sack the quarterback ten times, intercept five passes, block three punts, make a few touchdowns, and lead your team to win by forty-five points, I'm going to love you and be proud of you this much." I held my thumb and index finger about three inches apart to visually demonstrate my love for him. "I also want you to know that tonight, if you miss every tackle, miss every block, mess up every play, get benched, and cause your team to lose by fifty points, I'm still going to love you this much." Once again, I held my thumb and index finger the same three inches apart. I wanted my son to know that the measure of my love and acceptance would be the same in victory or defeat.

As soon as I said it, I knew I had hit a home run. I could see the stress, anxiety, and worry lift off his shoulders. I had spoken a relief of confidence and courage into his spirit and life. I had spoken words of boldness and inspiration to him and the result was noticeable immediately, in his countenance. He knew I loved and accepted him for who he was, and not for what he did. He believed the truth and did not accept the lie that performance earned love and acceptance.

When he got out of the car, I believe he could have run through a brick wall, he was so pumped and excited. In fact, he slammed the door so hard, my ears rang the whole way home. I knew that night would be a special night because a young teenager had heard and received words of truth and life, and it had set him free.

I'm not going to tell you who won the game or how many tackles he made or didn't make that night. It didn't matter. That night, Austen knew he was loved and accepted based on who he was, not on what he did. His earthly father was in the stands that night, proud as a peacock. Austen ended up being a great high school player and went on to get a scholarship to play football in Alabama. That night, though my ears were still ringing in pain from the slammed door, my heart was full. So is our Heavenly Father's heart full when His children hear His words of love and acceptance, life, and purpose.

An empty warehouse turns into clinics when we use the power of words. Empty clinic rooms are filled with doctors and patients when we use positive words to create what we want to see. Words are powerful keys to the beyond ordinary life. Show me the way you talk and I will show you your future.

Use your smartphone or tablet QR code reader to watch an important video about beyond ordinary living! Or, enter this link in your web browser: www.livingbeyondordinary.org/videos/chapter6.

Tweet these!

Describe a beyond ordinary encounter you've had. #beyondordinaryencounter http://bit.ly/1pVu3o1

Who are the encouraging, inspiring, positive voices surrounding you? #beyondordinaryvoices http://bit.ly/1pVu3o1

"It will always be a battle a day between those who want maximum change and those who want to maintain the status quo."—Gerry Adams

~

"I'm a harsh critic of the status quo."—Andrew Cuomo

~

"I hate to see complacency prevail in our lives when it's so directly contrary to the teaching of Christ."—Jimmy Carter

~

"I really try to put myself in uncomfortable situations. Complacency is my enemy."—Trent Reznor

~

"I think that one of the biggest flaws of mankind is that we become complacent with our lives."—Daniel Willey

~

"Courage, not compromise, brings the smile of God's approval."
—Thomas S. Monson

~

"Apathy in general; people who are not standing up for what they believe in because somebody's got a louder mouth than them; it doesn't make any sense."—Avan Jogia

~

"The manager accepts the status quo; the leader challenges it."
—Warren G. Bennis

~

"By far the most dangerous foe we have to fight is apathy—indifference from whatever cause, not from a lack of knowledge, but from carelessness, from absorption in other pursuits, from contempt bred of self satisfaction."
—William Osler

~

"Apathy is the glove into which evil slips its hand."—Bodie Thoene

~

"For the past 33 years, I have looked in the mirror every morning and asked myself: 'If today were the last day of my life, would I want to do what I am about to do today?' And whenever the answer has been 'no' for too many days in a row, I know I need to change something."—Steve Jobs

~

CHAPTER 7

BEYOND ORDINARY ACTIONS

"Actions speak louder than words" goes the well-turned phrase. That statement never became more relevant to me than in 2004, when we faced a very tough decision about the future of the mission in downtown Orlando. By this time, the mission was growing rapidly and helping hundreds of families every day. Although we were only a few years old, it was evident that our model and focus were working and we were onto something very special and unique.

Destiny Church had moved back to the Winter Park area, but the mission we had planted in downtown Orlando was still there: strong, vibrant, and expanding rapidly. As both pastor of a growing church and founder of the community outreach center, I was feeling the weight of leading both organizations effectively. Pastoring a local church is hard enough, let alone an innovative community center that was making a huge impact on the community and getting a lot of attention in the nonprofit world. Though both were very important to me, and up until then, I had been able to manage both, I knew one day I would have to let go of one so the other could grow and become all it was meant to be. A storm was brewing inside of me. The tension and stress of the daily demands of both, including the tremendous financial burden, were taking a toll, but I had no idea another storm was brewing on the horizon (#beyondordinarystorms).

The Storm(s) Hit

For the first time in recorded history, four major hurricanes hit Florida within just a two-month period, from August 13 through October 2, 2004. The "Big Four of 2004" all landed solidly in the list of costliest ever U.S. hurricanes. The devastating impact on the community was heartbreaking to see.

Florida Meets Charley

The eye of the worst hurricane to hit Florida in twelve years (the worst since Andrew in 1992) passed directly over and through Charlotte County, Florida, on Friday, August 13, 2004. Punta Gorda and Port Charlotte were flattened. The category four storm was far stronger than expected. When the eye reached Charlotte Harbor, the storm had punished the coastal communities with winds up to 145 mph and unleashed a storm surge of 13-15 feet. Orlando reported a peak sustained wind of 79 mph with a maximum gust to 105 mph. An F1 tornado ripped through the south side of Daytona Beach. The American Red Cross estimated one in three homes in Charlotte county—26,000—were destroyed or had major damage. In fact, Charley destroyed approximately 10,000 homes and left 16,000 with major damage.

Central Florida was devastated. Some who had been to war compared it to a war zone. Thousands of people suffered loss and were severely impacted by the storm. Needy families flocked to our center in numbers we had never seen before. It was pure crisis, but our staff and management team responded beautifully. Volunteers, corporations, churches, and the community all responded. Though many of them had been deeply and personally affected by this natural disaster, they reached out and helped us meet the demands of others more desperately in need. At the time, we had little idea of the financial impact Charley would have on our ministry, but we didn't really have time to think about that at the time, or to strategize. When a natural disaster hits, you react and do what needs to be done at the time. We did what we were called to do: help people.

"When a natural disaster hits, you react and do what needs to be done at the time. We did what we were called to do: help people."

In fact, this was the beginning of a dire financial crisis for us. The first revelation of this came when we were surprised to find that our insurance did not cover us for the food loss, damage, and our inability to officially open due to the loss of electricity. We opened our hearts to help thousands of people in need during the disaster, but because we opened our doors, we effectively disqualified ourselves from being able to make a claim on our policy—a huge mistake, apparently. It was nearly a knockout blow to the mission.

Heading to India Without a Clue

After weeks of emergency relief, confident we had a handle on the situation and that things were calming down a bit, I headed to Hyderabad, India, on a long-planned trip to conduct church services and community events. Knowing what I know now, I would never have gone, but at the time, it seemed everything was handled and under control. The staff and management team were stepping up and responding with compassion and heroic action. I felt obliged to fulfill my commitment to the event organizers in India, and was looking forward to ministering and expanding our influence in that country. I boarded the plane for India with full confidence in our team. I arrived in India on Saturday, September 3, 2004, after crossing many time zones on a long flight, made longer by delays. I slept the entire first day. When I awoke and turned on the TV, I was stunned at what I saw.

Florida Meets Frances

I was a world away, glued to CNN, and could not believe what I was seeing. Another major hurricane—Frances—was approaching Florida. The aerial images were shocking. It appeared to me the entire state would be covered. The smaller, compact Hurricane Charley had been so devastating, I couldn't imagine what this storm's potential would be.

Hurricane Frances made landfall in Florida on Sunday, September 5, 2004. She hit the east coast with 105 mph winds. Slow moving hurricanes are especially destructive, and Frances crawled along at only 7 mph, churning out destruction throughout the state. Frances was so enormous that she simultaneously affected the Florida Keys and pointed north into Georgia. She knocked out power across the state. Five million people in Florida would wait over a week for their power to be restored. The ferocity of the storm caused $10 billion in damage and took the lives of eighteen people in Florida.

Meanwhile, in India

There I was, on the other side of the world, hearing about this tragedy back home. I immediately tried to get back on a plane and head home, but the ticket cost $10,000. I attempted to call Tammi, but could not reach her. Between the great difference in time zones and the power shortage in Florida, it took many long hours before I was able to reach anyone in my family or on the leadership team of the church or mission. Finally, I made contact and was assured that my family, the church, and the mission were all well. Everyone I contacted back home in Florida encouraged me to stay in India and complete my mission.

Reluctantly, I stayed and finished my work in India, but it was the most difficult week of my life. The wonderful, kind people of India had no idea of the stress and fear I was facing on the inside. All they saw was an American pastor bringing a message of hope and help to their hungry nation. In fact, every minute was a struggle, as I wondered about my family, the church, the community center, and the families we helped each day. I was like a duck on water; calm and collected above the water line, paddling like crazy below it.

Florida Meets Hurricane Ivan

Ivan made landfall in Florida on Wednesday, September 15, 2004. Initially the most powerful of the storms, Ivan unleashed most of his category three fury on the Florida panhandle, after early predictions showed a path running through the middle of the peninsula. The estimated damage was $20 billion.

Florida Meets Hurricane Jeanne

The fourth hurricane to hit Florida in a six-week period, Hurricane Jeanne, made landfall on Saturday, September 25, 2004. At no time in recorded history had four hurricanes hit Florida in a single year, much less six weeks. Statewide, six people were killed. The estimated damage, insured and uninsured, was $12 billion.

Overall, approximately one of every five homes in Florida were damaged by the 2004 hurricane "train." Over two million insurance claims were filed. Needless to say, Florida was devastated and so was our downtown charity.

The Fallout of Another Big Storm

The direct effects and ripple effects were devastating for our charity. The entire region was in crisis mode for months and months. The number of people in need, just trying to survive, was at an all-time high. Staying afloat was a day-to-day struggle for them . . . and us. Nonprofits were sinking at an alarming rate, and so were the families they served—so they were coming to us. Donors were overwhelmed with the need, and donations we might normally have expected were sent to any number of other places.

Our supporters knew we were in crisis mode, but so were others. Every major national nonprofit was soliciting for emergency funds to help Floridians. We were still a very big nonprofit, but compared to the national charities, our voice and cries for help were not being heard. We just continued to do what we were called to do—help people—but the financial burden grew heavier and heavier. Unfortunately, we had little in reserve funds when the storms of 2004 began. By fall, we were several thousand dollars in debt, with few options and little time.

By early 2005, after much thought, prayer, and painful discussion, the Destiny Church leadership team arranged a succession plan for another church to oversee the Destiny Church ministries. They also decided that I would oversee the downtown Orlando mission, the Destiny Foundation ministry. However, this did not work out as planned, and we ultimately decided to dissolve and sell the Winter Park location to insure the viability of the Destiny Foundation.

This was not a popular decision many people simply didn't understand. Admittedly, I didn't do a great job communicating all of this and why we were doing it, due to the pressure I faced. I made many mistakes, mostly from trying to please everyone, and ended up failing to please many. Board members from the church and charity resigned. People were upset. Those closest to me knew my heart and intentions, and understood, but few others did. It was a very difficult situation to be in, and looking back, I certainly would have done things much differently if in the same situation today. At the time, action was needed, and our actions had to back up our talk—our promise to be there for our community. We had to prove the community center was in it for the long haul.

We've helped hundreds of thousands of people since we made that difficult decision to close one ministry so another could live. Though I lost friends because of the decision, ultimately, I have one person to answer to for my actions—God.

Though it wasn't a popular decision, I'm confident that in the long run, history will show that it was the best we could do in the midst of a storm.

"At the time, action was needed, and our actions had to back up our talk—our promise to be there for our community."

Lessons Learned in the Midst of the Storm

1. Storms will come.
2. We must stay true to our vision in the midst of storms.
3. Sometimes, we stand alone in taking decisive action in storms.
4. Heaven's presence will be with us in the storms.

The Stoning of Stephen

When the members of the Sanhedrin heard this, they were furious and gnashed their teeth at him. But Stephen, full of the Holy Spirit, looked up to heaven and saw the glory of God, and Jesus standing at the right hand of God. "Look," he said, "I see heaven open and the Son of Man standing at the right hand of God."

At this they covered their ears and, yelling at the top of their voices, they all rushed at him, dragged him out of the city and began to stone him. Meanwhile, the witnesses laid their coats at the feet of a young man named Saul.

While they were stoning him, Stephen prayed, "Lord Jesus, receive my spirit." Then he fell on his knees and cried out, "Lord, do not hold this sin against them." When he had said this, he fell asleep. (Acts 7:54-60, NIV)

Stephen faced a storm in his life. His storm came through the religious leaders of his day. They did not like Stephen. They didn't like his faith, his preaching, or the signs and wonders he did that confirmed for many the truth of his preaching. With courage and boldness, Stephen challenged the status quo of the culture of his day. He not only said some tough stuff, but he backed it up with action. The winds of criticism arose, the waves of jealousy grew bigger day by day, and suddenly, young Stephen was faced with hurricane force anger that led to his stoning.

In the face of opposition, Stephen became only more filled with passion and committed to action, even preaching to his adversaries and accusers. He realized the power of his heart having feet, and he backed up what he believed with movement. He was willing to die for his beliefs, something that came to the fore when his spirit of faith in action clashed with the status quo.

A Badge of Honor in the Storm of Life

Stephen's name means "badge of honor." I believe that when we stand up for God with more than just words, but actions, God stands up for us. This is the only time Scripture depicts Jesus standing. He's usually depicted sitting on His throne. However, when He finds great faith joined with action, He stands up and pins on the badge of honor.

Anybody can talk about what needs to be done; it takes a beyond ordinary leader to back it up with action—even unpopular action (#LivingBeyondOrdinary). We are all going to face storms in this life. Living beyond ordinary requires that when the storms of life come, we will stand with courage and conviction.

What Grandpa George Taught Me About the Storms of Life

I greatly admired my grandfather, James George. Though slight of stature, inwardly, he was a giant. As a ten-year-old boy, he was thrust into an awful storm. He and his father left Scotland by ship, and his mother and sister followed them to America. The journey was long and he quickly understood how hard storms can be. Halfway to America, his father (my great grandfather), took ill. He was quarantined and cared for by the medical team on the boat, leaving young James alone. Though he was told the separation would last only a few days, he quickly learned that once they arrived on Ellis Island, he would be isolated for nine months. Ten years old, separated from his father, he was alone among all the other refugees, awaiting their paperwork approval to gain access to a new life, or deportation back to Scotland.

"Living beyond ordinary requires that when the storms of life come, we will stand with courage and conviction."

I'm not really sure how bad it got for him, because Grandpa George was not comfortable talking about it. Whenever I asked him about details, he would quickly dismiss it and suddenly change the subject. Though we never really knew exactly what happened to him, I know for sure that whatever happened to him, he used it to become a great, great man. He was wise, cheerful, loving, compassionate, and loved God. These were character attributes he learned and developed while being alone and scared (#beyondordinarylessons).

After my grandfather passed away at the ripe old age of ninety-four, I had the opportunity to visit Ellis Island with my family. It was a very emotional experience for me to walk through the entire campus, to see and experience the place where he landed and made his entry into a new world. Considering the price he had to pay, the pain he had to endure, and the loss he had to experience, I couldn't help but wonder if he would do it all over again, if necessary. I believe he would. I believe he viewed the lessons learned in the storm to be far too valuable, somehow worth the suffering and pain.

When I was going through the worst storm of my life, Grandpa George's words often echoed in my head: "If you want to avoid the storms, say nothing, do nothing . . . and you will be nothing." Until I was in the midst of that storm, I had never fully understood what he meant. Thanks, Grandpa George, for your wisdom on facing the storms of my life.

Storms are painful. They were painful for me, they were painful for Stephen, they were painful for Grandpa George, and they will be painful for you. How we respond to them determines our growth, our future . . . our success in life. To live beyond ordinary, we must be willing to join faith with decisive action, even in the midst of the most difficult storms.

Use your smartphone or tablet QR code reader to watch an important video about beyond ordinary living! Or, enter this link in your web browser: www.livingbeyondordinary.org/videos/chapter7.

Tweet these!

What's the biggest storm you've faced in life? #beyondordinarystorms http://bit.ly/1pVu3o1

What lessons have you learned in the midst of your life's storms? #beyondordinarylessons http://bit.ly/1pVu3o1

"Good habits formed at youth make all the difference."—Aristotle

~

"I never could have done what I have done without the habits of punctuality, order, and diligence, without the determination to concentrate myself on one subject at a time."—Charles Dickens

~

"Successful people are simply those with successful habits."
—Brian Tracy

~

"The difference between an amateur and a professional is in their habits. An amateur has amateur habits. A professional has professional habits. We can never free ourselves from habit. But we can replace bad habits with good ones."—Steven Pressfield

~

"A change in bad habits leads to a change in life."—Jenny Craig

~

"The people you surround yourself with influence your behaviors, so choose friends who have healthy habits."—Dan Buettner

~

"The only proper way to eliminate bad habits is to replace them with good ones."—Jerome Hines

~

CHAPTER 8

BEYOND ORDINARY HABITS

Sue was a single mom with three sons. The former all-American cheerleader from Virginia never dreamed that her high school sweetheart, football star husband would pass away after twenty-one years of marriage. She had no idea he would leave her with no money and no plan. Sue heard she could move to Orlando and land a job, so she moved here, to "the city beautiful." She was right about landing a job, but what she didn't expect was that all the available jobs started at $7.25 an hour. With apartments renting at $842 per month for a two bedroom, she quickly found out how difficult her transition would be. To survive, she didn't need one job, but two.

Sue always dreamed of being a nurse—it was her life's calling. So as she worked two jobs and raised her sons, she also pursued a nursing degree. For over three years, Sue came to our campus regularly to receive food assistance, training, crisis services, and much more. She knew she could come to our campus and get a hand up and a little hope to give her strength to continue to fight.

At times, she showed up exhausted, and asked our staff members to pray for her, which they were glad to do. Other times, she needed a counselor to help her obtain other safety net services provided by local or state agencies. No matter the situation, Sue knew that when she set foot on our campus, she would be loved, respected, and find help. She would not be looked down on or frowned upon. Every week we would see her and encourage her to keep fighting.

There came a time when the staff noticed Sue was no longer coming in. Many of them had come to love her and missed seeing her on a weekly basis. Some thought she might have moved back to Virginia, fatigued and defeated. Sue put our wondering to rest one day when she walked into our center, her face bright and cheery, and asked for me. She was absolutely beaming she was so full of joy and confidence. She let me know that with our help, she had been able to graduate from nursing school and was working as a nurse at Florida Hospital, just a few miles away. Her children were doing well in school, life was getting back on track, and she wanted to personally thank me for our help. I'll never forget her next sentence: "One of my boys is in Boy Scouts, and as our way of saying thank you, he has taken on a service project. He wants to organize a food drive for you to help you continue to help others the way you helped us." Sue knew the power of healthy habits, and one of those is to give back. This was a tremendous blessing.

We Make Our Habits, and Our Habits Make Us

Sue practiced some very powerful habits in her life which motivated her to choose to rise above her circumstances and live beyond ordinary (#LivingBeyondOrdinary). Perhaps her mother or father taught and/or modeled them for her. Maybe she picked them up from a schoolteacher or Sunday school teacher. One way or another, she picked up the habits. So when Sue was at an all-time low, she reached down deep and pulled on those habits to navigate through her very difficult season of life. These habits helped her to break out of the mess she was in. She proved the truth of one of my favorite sayings: "We make our habits, and our habits make us." Sue built a new life through her beyond ordinary habits.

"We make our habits, and our habits make us."

Habit #1: Perseverance

When faced with grave adversity, Sue never quit. She never gave up. She never threw in the towel. Many times, people simply give up too soon. Those who have learned to persevere keep going, driven by the belief that they could be just one day away from a breakthrough, or just one week from a victory. Sue practiced the habit of perseverance and never lost her tenacity to fight. Even when she was tempted to stop, her belief that she was within striking distance of victory kept her going.

Habit #2: Responsibility

Sue could have blamed other people for her lot in life—her husband for not planning better, people who didn't hire her for the higher paying jobs, and others—but she didn't. Sue was determined not to play the blame game; she took personal responsibility for her own life and getting to the future she desired.

Habit #3: Forward Thinking

You cannot move forward while looking in the rearview mirror. Sue was determined not to be a prisoner of her past, but to move forward. I'm sure there were many times when she was tempted to look back with a "could of, would of, should of" mentality, but she was focused on her future. We all have things in our past we want to forget and move beyond. Like Sue, we need to practice forward thinking, keeping a laser beam focus on our positive vision for a bright future.

"Those who have learned to persevere keep going, driven by the belief that they could be just one day away from a breakthrough, or just one week from a victory."

Habits of Highly Effective People

Sadly, in over thirty years of ministry, helping tens of thousands of desperate people in need, I have found that most people we serve practice unhealthy, self-defeating habits. They have mastered the art of living with and accepting these habits. I am not saying their desperate situation is their fault, just that if they practiced healthy, life-affirming habits, it could make a great difference in their lives, for the better. We make our habits, and our habits make us.

In Stephen Covey's best-selling book, *The 7 Habits of Highly Effective People*, he expounds on habits successful people practice. Here's a brief recap of the habits he highlights:

Habit 1: Be Proactive

Take initiative in life by realizing that your life doesn't just happen, it is carefully designed by the choices and decisions you make. Proactive people are "response-able"—they take responsibility for their life, knowing it can be better by making better choices and decisions. This is a habit in which Sue excelled.

Habit 2: Begin with the End in Mind

This habit is based on the belief that everything is created twice, first in the mind, and then in the physical world. Get a vision for what you want in life and who you want to be and then be proactive in making decisions and choices that will get you there. This is exactly the forward thinking that Sue practiced.

Habit 3: Put First Things First

Focus first on things you, personally, find of most worth. Keep first things first: your purpose, values, roles, and priorities. Practice good life management by organizing and managing time and events according to the personal priorities you established in Habit 2.

Habit 4: Think Win-Win

Genuinely strive for mutually beneficial solutions or agreements in your relationships. Value and respect people by understanding a "win" for all is ultimately a better long-term resolution than if only one person in a given situation gets his or her way. "Win-win sees life as a cooperative arena, not a competitive one," wrote Covey.

Habit 5: Seek First to Understand, Then to Be Understood

Use empathic listening to be genuinely influenced by a person. This compels them to reciprocate the listening and take an open mind to being influenced by you.

Habit 6: Synergize

Creative cooperation is the key to synergy. By combining the strengths of people through positive teamwork, you will achieve goals no one person could have done alone.

Habit 7: Sharpen the Saw

Balance and renew yourself in the four areas of life—physical, social/emotional, mental, spiritual—and create a sustainable, long-term, effective lifestyle.[2]

7 Habits of Highly Ineffective People

In contrast to Covey's seven habits are my seven habits of people living self- defeating lives. These are negative actions, attitudes, and choices made by good people who are highly ineffective.

1. React

Instead of being proactive, ineffective people are continually reacting to circumstances in their life. They spend their life playing defense and catch up.

2. Begin with the Beginning in Mind

Ineffective people focus on what's at hand, not on what's down the road. They live day to day without regard for the future. They lack vision and a plan for a better life.

3. Put Last Things First

Ineffective people have priorities out of place and put their attention on things that really don't matter, or give the important and unimportant equal time and attention.

4. Think Win-Lose

Ineffective people live in a culture where someone must win and someone must lose (or where someone must lose for others to win). They can't wrap their minds around a win-win situation.

5. Seek First to Be Understood, Then to Understand

The habit of an ineffective person is that their sole goal is to be understood first, and then maybe understand. They talk rather than listen. Fear, insecurity, and failures in life create in them the goal of making sure people understand them first.

6. Isolate

Teamwork, collaboration, cooperation, and unity are foreign words to those who live inefficiently and ineffectively. They are survivors on a one-man island and are fighting the world all by themselves. They create division, drama, discord, disunity, and disharmony.

7. Dull the Blade

Highly ineffective people place a low priority on physical, social/ emotional, mental, and spiritual matters, such as prayer and meditation, being still, and listening. They are so busy surviving that they view this discipline as a waste of time.

I have made it my life's ambition to try to help people live effectively. After all, this book is titled *Living Beyond Ordinary* because that's what I want for you.

Habits I've Learned from Mistakes I've Made

We have all made mistakes that we regret. However, these mistakes can be huge opportunities for us to learn and develop good habits. I've learned that bad habits can be broken and new habits can be developed daily by making the decision to learn from our failures and mistakes. Here are three habits I've developed over the years (#beyondordinaryhabits):

Habit 1: Treat everyone with respect and dignity.

Habit 2: Don't overlook small details.

Habit 3: Treat each day like it's your last.

A visit to our campus by one family a few years ago proved why these habits are so crucial. It also reinforced the need for me to stay sharp, focused, and passionate.

The young family, a cute couple with a small child, met me in the parking lot as I was on my way to a very important meeting. They looked a bit lost and unsure of where to go, so I approached them and introduced myself to them. As soon as I said hello, they immediately recognized me. Apparently I had spoken at their church in nearby Lake County three years before. They remembered me talking about our mission in the sermon I'd preached. They said they felt impressed to come down for a look.

I was torn. On one hand, I had an important meeting to attend, off campus. On the other hand, I really enjoy showing people what we do. I'm like a proud daddy when it comes to showing off our programs and model for helping people, so I chose my heart and made a quick call that I'd be late for the meeting.

I'm so glad I did.

I said, "Come on, let me show you around." The tour went well, as most do, and after fifteen minutes, we were back in my office.

"We would like to help you out," they said.

Of course I said, "Great!"

They proceeded to pull out a check and started writing. I politely gave them some space and didn't look closely at what they were writing, but I did see the number 5. I thought to myself, *Maybe it's a $50 check . . . or $500.* It didn't matter. My passion was so strong and contagious that I never worried about how things would happen; I just knew when you do the right things, right things happen. They folded the check and handed it to me. I took it from them, put it in my pocket, prayed for them, and thanked them and God for their gift. The amount didn't matter to me. I wanted God and them to know that I was grateful. After our prayer, we hugged and I excused myself to leave for the meeting. We exchanged pleasant good-byes and I was off to attend to my duties for the rest of the day.

A Few Thousand Reasons to Be Thankful

I didn't think a thing about the check until later that night, after a long day. I got home and pulled the check out of my pocket. To my amazement and disbelief, the check was made out for $50,000! Not $5, $50, $500, or even $5,000 . . . but $50,000! I stood and looked at that check for what felt like an hour. I didn't talk and didn't move, I just stood in disbelief. After several minutes, I thought to myself,

This must be a mistake. This young couple in T-shirts, shorts, and ball caps couldn't have done this.

I quickly picked up my mobile phone, called them up, and cautiously thanked them for coming down that day and giving us the check. Then I asked them if this was a joke. I'm sure they thought I was a rookie fundraiser (which I was—still am). I surely don't get caught up in all the latest techniques and strategies used by professionals. To my relief, they said it was not a joke, laughed with me a minute, let me know how impressed they were, and wished me the very best. After the shock went away, my first reaction and thought was that I was glad I had developed healthy habits of treating everyone with respect, not overlooking minor details, and treating each day as if it were my last. These simple habits have served me well over the years and have proven to be most helpful in life, ministry, and in helping others live a life beyond ordinary (#LivingBeyondOrdinary).

Daniel's Highly Effective Habits

One of my favorite people in the Bible is Daniel. The name "Daniel" means, "God is my judge." Daniel realized that he only answered to one king—God. He had an audience of one in heaven and earth. Daniel had one tried and true habit that was birthed out of his values and gave him strength and purpose: daily prayer to God.

There came a time when the arrogant king of that day made a random law to prohibit all prayer in the land—that is, except prayer to him. Daniel was determined not to allow this law to override his values and habits, so he decided to continue to pray, regardless of the consequences. Here's the story:

> So these administrators and satraps went as a group
> to the king and said: "May King Darius live forever!
> The royal administrators, prefects, satraps, advisers

and governors have all agreed that the king should issue an edict and enforce the decree that anyone who prays to any god or human being during the next thirty days, except to you, Your Majesty, shall be thrown into the lions' den. Now, Your Majesty, issue the decree and put it in writing so that it cannot be altered—in accordance with the law of the Medes and Persians, which cannot be repealed." So King Darius put the decree in writing.

Now when Daniel learned that the decree had been published, he went home to his upstairs room where the windows opened toward Jerusalem. Three times a day he got down on his knees and prayed, giving thanks to his God, just as he had done before. Then these men went as a group and found Daniel praying and asking God for help. So they went to the king and spoke to him about his royal decree: "Did you not publish a decree that during the next thirty days anyone who prays to any god or human being except to you, Your Majesty, would be thrown into the lions' den?"

The king answered, "The decree stands—in accordance with the law of the Medes and Persians, which cannot be repealed."

Then they said to the king, "Daniel, who is one of the exiles from Judah, pays no attention to you, Your Majesty, or to the decree you put in writing. He still prays three times a day." When the king heard this, he was greatly distressed; he was determined to rescue Daniel and made every effort until sundown to save him.

Then the men went as a group to King Darius and said to him, "Remember, Your Majesty, that according to the law of the Medes and Persians no decree or edict that the king issues can be changed."

So the king gave the order, and they brought Daniel and threw him into the lions' den. The king said to Daniel, "May your God, whom you serve continually, rescue you!"

A stone was brought and placed over the mouth of the den, and the king sealed it with his own signet ring and with the rings of his nobles, so that Daniel's situation might not be changed. Then the king returned to his palace and spent the night without eating and without any entertainment being brought to him. And he could not sleep.

At the first light of dawn, the king got up and hurried to the lions' den. When he came near the den, he called to Daniel in an anguished voice, "Daniel, servant of the living God, has your God, whom you serve continually, been able to rescue you from the lions?"

Daniel answered, "May the king live forever! My God sent his angel, and he shut the mouths of the lions. They have not hurt me, because I was found innocent in his sight. Nor have I ever done any wrong before you, Your Majesty."

The king was overjoyed and gave orders to lift Daniel out of the den. And when Daniel was lifted from the den, no wound was found on him, because he had trusted in his God.

At the king's command, the men who had falsely accused Daniel were brought in and thrown into the lions' den, along with their wives and children. And before they reached the floor of the den, the lions overpowered them and crushed all their bones. (Daniel 6:6-24, NIV)

Daniel practiced a few other healthy habits he had learned to live by that served him well and helped him live a beyond ordinary life. These would be good for all of us to learn.

Habit 1: Daniel practiced fearlessness.

Daniel knew he had only one judge, so he feared no one. Every time he heard his name ("God is my judge"), it reminded him to live life without the fear of man.

So many people I meet live their lives in constant fear of what others may think. They are so consumed with the opinions of others that they live their entire lives to please them. I love the confidence of Daniel. He was determined to live for the applause of one. When you make the decision to develop the habit of living fearlessly—free from the fear of what others think—you will be one step closer to living a beyond ordinary life.

"When you make the decision to develop the habit of living fearlessly—free from the fear of what others think—you will be one step closer to living a beyond ordinary life."

Habit #2: Daniel asked for help.

Daniel needed help. He was in a tough situation and needed someone to give him a hand. Daniel realized the power of asking for help, through prayer. This habit of continually depending on His God for strength, wisdom, and peace, enabled him to live a victorious life. People want to help. Our community is filled with people who want to help—they just need to be asked. When you discover the freedom of the realization that you do not have to do it all yourself (or that not just you alone can do it), people will step up in your life and help you in your time of need, simply because you asked for help.

Habit #3: Daniel stayed the course.

It would have been easy for Daniel to get off track and give in to the king's request to stop his prayers, but he had learned the value of staying on track and not budging from his convictions and beliefs.

Our society today is full of wishy-washy people who are out of tune with their convictions, and therefore, cannot stay the course in times of pressure and testing. I love the fact that Daniel valued his beliefs and was willing to stand against the world, if necessary, to stay true to them. Because of the habits he practiced, this highly effective man of God lived a beyond ordinary life.

We make our habits, and our habits make us. Do you want to change your life? Change your habits. To live a life beyond ordinary, you need to practice beyond ordinary habits. What habits will you start today to begin your beyond ordinary life?

Use your smartphone or tablet QR code reader to watch an important video about beyond ordinary living! Or, enter this link in your web browser: www.livingbeyondordinary.org/videos/chapter8.

Tweet these!

What habits have you developed that help you live beyond ordinary? #beyondordinaryhabits http://bit.ly/1pVu3o1

What habits do you need to develop to live beyond ordinary? #beyondordinaryhabits http://bit.ly/1pVu3o1

"Character cannot be developed in ease and quiet. Only through experience of trial and suffering can the soul be strengthened, ambition inspired, and success achieved."—Helen Keller

~

"Be more concerned with your character than your reputation, because your character is what you really are, while your reputation is merely what others think you are."—John Wooden

~

"Character may be manifested in the great moments, but it is made in the small ones."—Phillips Brooks

~

"I look to a day when people will not be judged by the color of their skin, but by the content of their character."
—Dr. Martin Luther King, Jr.

~

"Character develops itself in the stream of life."
—Johann Wolfgang von Goethe

~

"Character is what a man is in the dark."—Dwight L. Moody

~

"Character isn't something you were born with and can't change, like your fingerprints. It's something you weren't born with and must take responsibility for forming."—Jim Rohn

~

"This is the very perfection of a man, to find out his own imperfections."—Saint Augustine

~

CHAPTER 9

BEYOND ORDINARY CHARACTER

I waited to write this chapter until close to the end because of the extreme pain and heartache I still feel over this event, even five years later. It was the loss of a dream . . . the death of a vision. I am still not sure why it occurred and believe I may only know in eternity. To this day, I still have not recovered from it. One thing I do know is that, like any individual or organization that would strive to live beyond ordinary, our story includes many highs and some depressing lows. However, I will quickly add that even through the lowest of lows, we have always remained committed to bringing good to the lives of people going through the worst of times.

Extraordinary Economic Collapse

In the fall of 2008, along with the rest of America, we began seeing some warning signs that the economy was in trouble, but had no idea the depth of the trouble and the ripple effect of it on us. In spite of growing concern, we closed out 2008 ahead of budget, having made tremendous headway in serving our community. However, in the back of our minds, we weren't as confident heading into the new year as we had been in the past.

The new year started off with a bang. Donations were up and we wondered if our concerns had been unwarranted. Then they suddenly dropped off . . . like a cliff. The second obvious sign that things were beginning to crumble was the scarcity of food on the secondary market. To say that we quickly felt the U.S. economic collapse would be an understatement.

No one knew that the greatest U.S. economic crisis since the Great Depression was upon us (#beyondordinaryrecession). Families were flocking to food banks across America in record numbers. Families that had never before needed food were now lining up.

The food bank system throughout the U.S. had never seen the demand it saw in 2009, and for some time thereafter. Food that had always been available for us to purchase for the food bank was suddenly non-existent. Almost overnight, the food disappeared, and try as we did, we could not find new sources for it. Since our model relied heavily on food being available to our working poor families, through our cost-share grocery program, our need was desperate. We were slammed with children and families in need of food and had nothing for them. At time, the demand was triple that of previous years as the number of needy families multiplied. Just as the food disappeared and the demand tripled, our donations went off the cliff. It was the perfect storm.

The Perfect Storm

At the time, even our must dependable and generous donors were unable to help us pull out of our nosedive. Still, we were committed to pressing on, somehow, to help families see good in their worst times.

Our board of directors and leadership team were engaged, strategizing to keep our ship afloat, but the water was rushing in so fast, we struggled to find hope we could salvage our vessel. We were also in the middle of an executive director transition at the time, so that didn't make things any easier. Any change can be a challenge, but a time of severe crisis is about the worst time to undergo a key leadership transition. In hindsight, this proved to be the issue that sunk our ship. We were a very big ship. Like all big ships, it was impossible to change direction quickly—at least not quickly enough. Also, big ships sink fast. We saw this firsthand.

The Beyond Ordinary Team

Our board was comprised of brilliant businesspeople. Many of them led their own companies. In fact, a few of them were in executive leadership positions at some of the largest companies in Central Florida. They were trusted, seasoned business leaders, helping to lead a charity that only a few months before had been on top of the world, but was now sinking—and sinking fast. This dedicated team had never experienced anything like this before. So not only did 2009 present uncharted waters for our nation, state, and city, but for our charity. We did the very best we could in very, very difficult times. After all, during that season, banks, corporations, and financial institutions that had been around for even 100 years were falling left and right. Companies some thought would never fall did.

Seeing this happen around us did not help to boost our confidence. It was scary to see and even scarier to experience. We made all the necessary adjustments to reduce our expenses and cut costs, but the volume of people coming to us was multiplying at such a rate, we couldn't keep up. We were depleting our reserves and our team couldn't raise enough money to keep up. The small amount of funds that came in went right back out just as quickly, being spent on meeting needs. Every day that food was unavailable, we slipped further and further into despair.

Some said we cared too much and felt too great a responsibility (as if that were possible). All we knew to do as the need multiplied was increase and multiply our efforts. We just kept giving and giving. It was impossible to say no to families that were struggling in the economic meltdown. One of the hardest things to see was some of our most faithful donors turn into clients, right before our eyes. Nothing could have prepared us for what we were seeing on an hourly basis. Every day we thought it couldn't get any worse, but every new day revealed it could.

Tough Decisions of Beyond Ordinary Friends

The board members were all close friends and associates of mine. Many of them had worked with me for years. In many cases, even our children were friends. We were neighbors who enjoyed watching our son's baseball games together. We were involved in some of the same church activities and so much more. We had developed deep relationships. I was grateful for their leadership and friendship, but now the storm we were in would test these relationships.

As founder and president, though I had no voting power on any decisions that were about to be made (and technically, was not a board member), I was ultimately responsible. Years before, the board made the decision for me to lead the ministry, but not hold a board position, as we wanted to meet the highest standards in the nonprofit world and be above reproach in every area. This may have been a fatal mistake on my part. However, given the same circumstances, even now, I don't believe I would be able to navigate through that difficult storm. It was truly an impossible situation. Still, then just as now, I am willing to take any and all blame for what took place under my watch.

At the time these decisions were made, the board was holding meetings to which I was not invited.

I remember a board member patting me on the back, saying: "Don't worry, Scott. We will always have your back and your best interests at heart." Nevertheless, by that time, panic had set into my heart and mind to a degree I have no words to describe: "despair" doesn't even come close. After having poured all my heart, soul, and a great amount of personal finance into the mission, the board was making major decisions without my input or advice. The beautiful young organization had been thrown into a hurricane, and sadly, I knew it was only a matter of days before the closing would eventually happen. Happen, it did.

"The beautiful young organization had been thrown into a hurricane, and sadly, I knew it was only a matter of days before the closing would eventually happen."

Late one night, the board called Tammi and me to the downtown Orlando boardroom to tell us their decision. I remember the drive from our Maitland home to the boardroom was very long and quiet. I knew that the decision the board had made would affect literally thousands and thousands of people. Although I was really scared for us, I was more deeply concerned for the families that counted on us.

When we walked in, I could see the stress and turmoil on the face of each board member. I was very sorry for having put them in this position. Many of them had given generously: all were all-in. I knew they were deeply troubled by the decision they had made: they simply felt they had no options left. I would never have asked them to be a part of the organization had I known the pain and turmoil it would have put them through.

The meeting was direct and very emotional: They were closing down the Destiny Foundation.

Afterwards, we were both numb and in shock. We could not believe it had come down to this. This was the most painful experience we had ever experienced—a deep sick feeling that stuck with us for a long time. Awake or asleep, it was there, I could not escape it. All I had preached about pain, suffering, turmoil, and enduring it through faith in God . . . I now had to practice all of it in the face of the biggest battle of my life.

The Aftermath

The next morning, after a long sleepless night, my first duty of the day was to address the local media. As much as I wanted to run and hide, I knew it was my responsibility to face them with my head held high. There was nothing to hide—no scandal and no accusations. It had all been a matter of bad timing and an unprecedented economic crisis. Looking back, it is ironic that although I was not involved in the decision-making process, I was the one answering all the questions: It would be my face on the front page of the local newspaper. Part of me wanted the board members to answer to the media instead. I remember thinking: *They ultimately made the final decision to close the Destiny Foundation. Let them field the tough questions and face the newspaper reporters.* That didn't happen. However, I wasn't running. I mustered up all the courage I possibly could and faced the music.

In years past, I had grown used to waking up, walking down my driveway, and picking up the *Orlando Sentinel* newspaper to find positive reports on our organization right there on the front page. The day after the interview, I was not prepared to make the same walk, just to open up the newspaper and see myself on the front page, announcing the closing. Not only was the article gut-wrenching to read, the picture they decided to run was even more telling. Of all the pictures they could have used, the one they chose to publish was the one of me on the steps of our multimedia area, my face down in my hands. I still have that picture: I keep it handy as a reminder—just a few inches away from my office desk. Every once in a while, I look over at that picture to remind me of that painful season in my life and find renewed strength to face current challenges.

The article in the *Orlando Sentinel* hit me hard and left me in shock—shock similar to what you feel after someone dear to you has died, and you remember it and relive it. It was a very good, fair article that simply explained our situation in a factual manner. The reporter was very aware of who we were and what we did as she had covered us many times. I am sure it was perplexing and difficult for her to report our sad news.

As difficult as the closing was, the most painful part was not answering the media or discussions with our loyal donors: it was letting go of the staff and the silence of the board during all of this. What Dr. Martin Luther King, Jr., once said was true: "In the end, we will remember not the words of our enemies, but the silence of our friends." I found this to be true. Once the board made their decision and I was thrust into the media spotlight, they were silent, and it saddened me. I try to understand this. I realize they were scared, fearful—and some, embarrassed. They didn't know what to do, so they reacted in fear and this fear caused them to avoid my family and me.

The board knew that their decision would affect my family's financial future in a very big way. I had loaned the foundation several hundred thousand dollars to get them through difficult times and I was on the line for debts from the charity. I had mortgaged my cars to help the charity. I was penniless, without even an automobile to my name. Just a few months before this, our organization was helping hundreds of unemployed workers a day. Now, I was filling out unemployment paperwork, needing help myself.

Years later, as Tammi and I stood in the parking lot of the Community Food and Outreach Center (formerly the Destiny Foundation) a former board member was brave enough to at least have a conversation with me. He said he was embarrassed and ashamed of what had happened. He felt terrible and was very uncomfortable being back on the campus. He has not returned since then. Dr. King's words again echoed in my head.

Godly Character

David was known as many things—a humble shepherd, a victorious warrior, an anointed psalmist, Israel's greatest king, a champion over Goliath—but his greatest attribute was that he desired to be a man of godly character. God even described David as a man after His own heart. Here is a portion of a psalm of David that reveals his heart: "Create in me a pure heart, O God, and renew a steadfast spirit within me. Do not cast me from your presence or take your Holy Spirit from me. Restore to me the joy of your salvation and grant me a willing spirit, to sustain me" (Psalms 51:10-12, NIV).

It may be shocking to learn that when David penned Psalm 51, he was just emerging from a terrible season of sin and betrayal. He was guilty of lies and worse. He had committed adultery with a woman, Bathsheba, when her husband was away at war. He tried to cover it up, but when Bathsheba found she was pregnant, David made sure the generals put her husband, a fellow general, on the front lines of a battle and abandoned him there, leaving him to be killed by the enemy.

How was this possible for David, a man after God's own heart? How can each of us fail or make the grave mistakes we do, at times? I'm not sure we will ever fully understand why. Even theologians and Bible experts have no sufficient explanation.

What fascinates me about this story is how David, in the midst of his confession and repentance, cried out for a clean heart. His focus was on the desperate condition of his heart and its restoration. His prayer emerged from renewed character.

You can learn a lot about yourself when your life falls apart. A person with the right heart and character will learn, grow, and move forward. How we respond at such times determines our future.

"You can learn a lot about yourself when your life falls apart. A person with the right heart and character will learn, grow, and move forward. How we respond at such times determines our future."

Lessons Learned from Painful Times

In life, there are some lessons we can learn only during times of great challenge, suffering, or pain. I have learned a number of valuable lessons for living beyond ordinary, through the most difficult times in my life (#LivingBeyondOrdinary).

1. Everyone faces difficult seasons.

You cannot genuinely live life without having to face tough times. It's not a matter of if, but only when difficult times will come your way. You will be known for and remembered by how you respond to difficulty (#beyondordinarylessons). Even when life is at its most painful and perplexing, you must be mindful of the many people who are counting on you to respond properly.

2. Your destiny will be determined by how you react to tough times.

In the midst of terrible times, you must look forward. Your future depends on—and is largely determined by—how you respond to lonely seasons and tough times.

3. It's about what's happening in you, not around you that really matters.

God will use even the most difficult of situations to develop your heart and character—to cause you to grow. What happens to your heart is most important. It is very hard not to react negatively to the painful and perplexing events in your life. The temptation to immerse yourself in sadness, to wallow in helplessness, and to struggle for answers can be extreme. This is when it is most important to focus on the good that can happen in you through the pain and struggle—to be determined to be made stronger and come out better for it.

"You will be known for and remembered by how you respond to difficulty (#beyondordinarylessons)."

---

4. Although you feel alone, you will always have a friend.

Many times, when we are faced with painful situations, we can feel totally alone and isolate ourselves from others. It's at just such times that we can count on God's presence to fill us with courage and peace, if we seek Him. David cried out for God's presence to never leave him and God became his closest friend and most reliable confidant. Expect God to reveal close friends to you at such times. Though many of the people you think or wish would be there will not be, other close friends will be, and they will surprise you with their kindness and compassion.

5. God is more concerned with your character than He is with your comfort.

During hard seasons of life, God's primary focus is on your heart and character. Your comfort is not His top priority. When you begin to realize that God is using these circumstances to shape your heart and character, it helps you make sense of the crazy things happening around you (though you may not ever fully understand them).

6. Run to God, not from Him.

In hard times, whether out of anger, fear, or disappointment, many people choose to run from God. David had learned the secret of running to God in difficult times. At the worst time, ask Him to give you courage and strength. One of my favorite scriptures during my life's most difficult season was, "I call as my heart grows faint; lead me to the rock that is higher than I" (Psalm 61:2, NIV).

I encourage you to run to God in difficult times. He is a rock you can stand on, a place of refuge for you—a shelter from the storm. As you stand firm, looking through the storm to the good that will come, He will forge your character, refine and purify you, and strengthen you with resilience to stand ever stronger. This is a vital key to living a beyond ordinary life.

Use your smartphone or tablet QR code reader to watch an important video about beyond ordinary living! Or, enter this link in your web browser: www.livingbeyondordinary.org/videos/chapter9.

Tweet these!

What lessons did you learn from the economic meltdown of 2009? #beyondordinaryrecession http://bit.ly/1pVu3o1

What is the most valuable lesson you've learned from a difficult time in life? #beyondordinarylessons http://bit.ly/1pVu3o1

"The opportunity of a lifetime must be seized within the lifetime of the opportunity."—Leonard Ravenhill

~

"Our lives are a series of defining moments, strung together by passing time. Surrender fully to this moment, because it is not the moment itself that defines us, but how we choose to live in it."
—Jill Pendley

~

"I wouldn't trade any of the rotten times. They're vital to defining who you are and what you want."—Anatole France

~

"When a defining moment comes along, you can do one of two things. Define the moment, or let the moment define you."
—*Tin Cup*, movie

~

"The secret of success in life is for a man to be ready for his opportunity when it comes."—Benjamin Disraeli

~

CHAPTER 10

BEYOND ORDINARY DESTINY

Our lives are made up not of years, months, weeks, or minutes . . . but of moments. These moments define us. Everyone has them, and you can probably recall a few of yours: moments when you suddenly viewed yourself, others, the world, or even God differently. These defining moments help shape our character, and character prepares us to shine in tough times. The greater our character, the more brightly we shine—even in the darkest times.

Some defining moments are once in a lifetime, when suddenly, everything in our lives changes. On January 15, 2009, Captain Chesley Burnett "Sully" Sullenberger, III, had just such a defining moment when he successfully executed the emergency water landing of his stricken U.S. Airways airliner on the Hudson River. All 155 passengers and crew members survived. Later on, Captain Sullenberger would say that he had been preparing his entire career for that one defining moment. Characteristic of defining moments, Sullenberger had no time to decide the kind of man he would be or to reflect on and consider how to react. The man he was came out. He was ready and responded with the clarity, conviction, and courage he had developed for years (#LivingBeyondOrdinary).

"When the moment's right . . . will you be ready?"

We have all seen the erectile dysfunction (ED) commercials on TV. Apparently they are a big sponsor of *Sports Center* on ESPN, because every time I watch that show or a basketball game, every other commercial seems to be about ED. This is especially awkward as my daughters always seem to enter the room when these crazy ads come on. An especially crazy thing about these commercials is that they actually ask a very important question of us all—not about our sex lives, but about our destiny—"When the moment's right, will you be ready?" When that defining moment suddenly arises, will you be ready? We can learn a lot from both those who were ready for their moment . . . and a few who were not (#beyondordinarydefiningmoment).

Thrill of Victory and Agony of Defeat

When I was growing up, every Saturday I watched *Wide World of Sports* with Tim McKay, on ABC. This was before ESPN, and if you were into sports, this was the show to watch. I loved the opening and the music when he said, "The thrill of victory . . ." and then, ". . . and the agony of defeat." As McKay said, "The thrill of victory," the images on TV were of inspiring, iconic victories: boxers celebrating and baseball players crying in their big moment. However, these inspiring scenes of victory were then followed by the five dreaded words, "and the agony of defeat," at which point the music turned suddenly darker and images of grave defeats were shown. One of these, I will never be able to get out of my mind. It was a short clip of a long jump skier hurtling down the ski ramp when just before he's set to shoot high into the sky, he tumbles, becoming a spinning, jumbling heap, flipping and flopping all the way down the side of the ski slope. His skis flew one way while his body flew the other. It was a mess to watch—an awesome mess to watch. This guy was clearly and utterly experiencing the agony of defeat. For twenty-five years, this was the consummate image of defeat for many of us.

Not much was said of this skier for a long time. He didn't have a nametag on the back of his ski suit and, until writing this chapter and the phrase "the agony of defeat" came to me, I hadn't thought much about this. As I thought about the emotion and pain of that moment and what defeat was like, I decided to do a little research on the skier who made famous the phrase, "the agony of defeat."

Vinko Bogataj's Defining Moment

Vinko Bogataj was the name of that infamous, unfortunate skier. He was competing as a Yugoslavian entrant at the Ski-Flying World Championships in Oberstdorf, West Germany (now Germany), on March 7, 1970. A light snow had begun falling at the start of the event, and by the time Bogataj was ready for his third jump, the snow had become quite heavy. Midway down the ramp for that jump, Bogataj realized that the conditions had made the ramp too fast. He attempted to lower his center of gravity and stop his jump, but instead, lost his balance completely and rocketed out of control off the end of the ramp, tumbling and flipping wildly, and crashing through a light retaining fence near a crowd of stunned spectators before coming to a halt. Despite the ferocity of the crash, Bogataj suffered only a mild concussion.

Bogataj returned to ski jumping the next year, but never duplicated the success he had before the crash and retired from the sport competitively (except for occasional senior competitions thereafter). During his career, Bogataj's best career finish was 57th in the individual normal hill event at Bischofshofen, Austria, in 1969, during that year's Four Hills Tournament.

Bogataj became a ski instructor, coaching the 1991 World Champion Slovenian ski jumper, Franci Petek, and supplementing his income by painting and operating a forklift at a factory.

It is likely that Vinko Bogataj's crash would have remained obscure had a film crew from *Wide World of Sports* not been on hand to record the event. The show featured an opening narration (by host Jim McKay) over a montage of sports clips, and coordinating producer Dennis Lewin inserted the footage of Bogataj's tremendous tumble to coincide with the words, "...and the agony of defeat." Throughout the show's long history, various images were used for the other parts of the narration, including for "The thrill of victory..." which directly preceded the above phrase and was often accompanied by images of the celebrating team at the most recent Super Bowl or World Cup. But for those many years after that point, the "agony of defeat" was always illustrated by Bogataj's failed jump.

The melodrama of the narration—which became a catchphrase in the US—and the sympathetic pain of watching Bogataj wipe out week after week, transformed the unaccredited ski jumper into an American icon of bad luck and misfortune. Meanwhile, having retired to his quiet, private life in Slovenia, Vinko Bogataj was unaware of his celebrity status, and so was quite confused when he was asked to attend the 20th anniversary celebration for Wide World of Sports in 1981. He was stunned when other more famous athletes present, such as Muhammad Ali, asked him for his autograph.

Today, Bogataj still lives in his home town of Lesce, Slovenia. He is married and has two daughters.[3]

When asked about it, Bogataj was quoted as saying, "Every time I'm on ABC, I crash." Vinko not only survived, but was able to walk away from that terrible crash. He then became famous for his infamous fall. His loss became a huge gain for him and millions of people watching that program because, in a weird way, he inspired and motivated us. If Vinko can get up and walk away from that crash in the face of his agony of defeat, we can get up and walk on from falls, failures, and crashes. I love the fact that he got up and walked away and the end of his story was not failure, loss or defeat, but victory and success.

Vinko's defining moment was his reaction and response to falling: he got up and lived a life in many ways better than he had ever known. Like Vinko, we rarely understand the gravity of the defining moments we are in. However, when they come, we must be ready.

Our Defining Moment

The closing of the Destiny Foundation was front page news. Though it was an unbelievably difficult time for me, I did not have time to wallow in self-pity or complain. People were still in need, and they weren't caught up in the drama and news—most of them couldn't even afford a newspaper. They weren't immersed in the complexities of what was going on legally or politically. All they knew was that life had thrown them a curve ball—again—and their struggle was made that much worse.

During this "transition" for me, I remember one of our clients pulling me aside and saying: "Pastor Scott, there are a lot of people who are panicked and confused about what has happened. They are scared! So many people are counting on you." Those words really shook me. After all, my life was in shambles and falling apart, but there were tens of thousands who were in worse shape than I was, for sure. I didn't need added pressure at that point in my life, but I did need to be reminded that this was not about me . . . it was about them. Whatever I needed to do, it was now time to see what I was really "made of." It was time to fight again . . . and my, what a fight it would be.

From the minute the Destiny Foundation doors closed, I was determined that the vision would still remain. I didn't understand how it would be possible, and lacked the faith to believe it could happen, but I still had the fight in me and I was willing to let go.

Two Beyond Ordinary Friends

Shortly after we started the mission in Orlando, we heard about a young man, Austin Hunt, who was doing a ministry similar to ours in the Fort Pierce area, a few hours south of Orlando. We began to talk and eventually began working together in partnership. We attended conferences together, worked together on mission trips, and connected on various ministry opportunities. Most importantly, we developed a friendship over many years.

A few days after the crisis in Orlando started, I began getting calls from Austin, checking on me and encouraging me in my season of discouragement. Austin had once sat on our Destiny Foundation board of directors, providing invaluable insight, expertise, leadership, and wisdom. Then his ministry grew and serving on our board was no longer an option for him. Now, in the midst of my crisis, he was there for me, filled with faith and encouragement. Although the economy had affected him greatly as well, he didn't want to simply give up and walk away from what he had helped build in Orlando. Austin encouraged me to not give up and helped motivate me to believe that we could resurrect the ministry. Though I was emotionally drained and exhausted, every time he called, he stirred the desire in me not to quit on the dream. Austin knew as well as I did that way too many great things had happened for our city through our mission, so we couldn't just give up and walk away.

I've known Andrae Bailey for fifteen years, first meeting him during my days as pastor of Destiny Church. Andrae attended

Destiny Church for some time before serving as its executive pastor for many years. After our time together in church work, he became the executive director for the Destiny Foundation. Months prior to the closing of the Destiny Foundation, Andrae went south to continue to work with Austin Hunt in Ft. Pierce and Vero Beach, doing the same type of work we were doing in Orlando. Andre, Austin, and me had worked very closely together. We were pioneers in this particular area of nonprofit and we needed each other. Daily, we would call each other for help, encouragement, and wisdom.

Andrae is a fighter and a master strategist with a unique ability to navigate through difficult situations with wisdom and tenacity. I often call him the "Karl Rove" of nonprofit work. (Rove served as chief strategist in the successful presidential campaigns of George W. Bush in 2000 and 2004.) He has a huge heart and is one of the few people I would want in the bunker with me in battle. In fact, we have fought many battles together. His loyalty is humbling and I am grateful for it. I never knew the depth of his loyalty until it was time to rebuild.

Andrae Bailey and Austin Hunt

Because Andrae had worked so closely with me and knew all the details about this ministry, he was the first one I called when I knew things were going south and the Destiny Foundation was about to close. Andrae is such a fighter; he refused to let the ministry die. He immediately contacted Austin Hunt and started to cast the vision for a rebirth of the mission. It was an emotionally exhausting time, yet in the midst of all the pain, Andrae Bailey still had the vision and the fight to do all in his power to keep the ministry alive. I give him all the credit in the world for never giving up, and for bringing everyone together to launch the Community Food and Outreach Center. In that very dark season, he was the only person who really saw the potential and opportunity. He pulled on all his resources and contacts to make it happen. In a season when

I was just trying to hold things together, Austin was down south fighting for the dream. He was resolved and determined, a fearless fighter on behalf of people in need in Central Florida.

We didn't have much time, so decisions were made quickly. A plan was beginning to take shape and things had begun to fall into place. Austin's board moved quickly and confidently, securing sufficient funding for us to re-launch and reopen the campus. In many regards, we had to start from scratch; but in many others, due to the already laid foundation, we picked up quickly from where Destiny Foundation left off. Many partners and donors were back on board immediately, though for some, it took a few months. For others, it was just too big of a roller coaster ride, and they needed some time. One thing was certain, we had to fight and claw our way through. We were tenacious and determined. My alliance with Andrae and Austin made us all stronger and better.

The Thrill of Victory

My family could not have survived this tragedy without the generous support of friends, family, our home church and community. Literally, within hours of the news of the close of Destiny Foundation, our neighbors in the Kings Row subdivision started dropping off cards filled with gift cards and condolences. Friends showed up at our house in tears and disbelief. The recession of 2009 had found its way into our small Orlando suburb and the pain was real and heartfelt. Our home church, First United Methodist Church, sent pastors to pray for us and gifts to help us move forward. The kindness expressed was overwhelming and so appreciated. Our neighbors were concerned about the impact on our children, so they dropped off gift cards for them for everything from Starbucks to movies. The athletic director at our children's Christian school in Maitland, Orangewood, reached out in compassion and helped us by eliminating fees for sports and extracurricular activities which helped to soften the blow that was about to come to our entire family. Gift baskets arrived within days, with cards of sympathy from people we didn't really know, expressing their kindness in unexpected ways. For months, I would be in a restaurant and people would unexpectedly pick up my check, and not just once or twice, but probably 15-20 times. It was like the community saying to me and my family, "Thank you for what you have done."

There are so many people I was unable to thank during this troubling time, but I want to take time in this book to thank you now. I may never be able to personally thank you and communicate effectively the peace and security you brought, not only to my wife and I, but our children as well. For those of you who dropped off gifts or picked up the tab at a restaurant, thank you! To those who made sure my children had the little things that are important to teens during that time, thank you! For those who prayed and supported us with words of encouragement and inspiration, thank you for lifting us up! We felt every prayer and appreciated every act of kindness. I will never forget and I will always be full of gratitude for all of this.

The reaction in the community was overwhelmingly positive and encouraging. People love to see comeback stories, and ours certainly was a great one. All said and done, we were closed for only a few days.

"People love to see comeback stories, and ours certainly was a great one."

Finally, I have to say that thousands of families have been helped because of the fight and vision of Andrae Bailey and Austin Hunt. I am *forever* grateful for their friendship, passion, and determination. Our community is better because of them. Struggling families have hope because of them. Children have food because of them. I am a better leader and man because of them.

Austin and Andrae taught me to fight, to tenaciously battle for what I believed in, and to never give up. The three of us have continued being pioneers together, blazing new trails into new frontiers. We have made a few enemies along the way, typically people who want to maintain the status quo, who do not want change and progress: people who think more about themselves than of those who are struggling. Yet we have made far more friends and developed incredible relationships.

At the time of this writing, Andrae had just accepted a position on the regional homeless commission in our tri-county area. He has been an incredible voice and advocate for homeless children and families in Central Florida. I'm very proud of him. Hopefully, I've had even half the impact on him that he has had on me. Austin and I are still working together very closely, establishing community centers in our state and beyond. We currently have three sites in Florida and are looking to expand into other cities as opportunities arise.

Facts About Defining Moments

Through the closing of the Destiny Foundation and launching of the Community Food and Outreach Center, I learned quite a bit about defining moments as I lived through mine.

1. Everyone has defining moments.

Every single person alive will have defining moments; some more than others, but we will all have our share. Our future is determined by how we respond to these very special moments in our lives.

2. You never really know when your defining moments will be.

You must be ready and prepared because you never know exactly when they will come. When they do come, you may not recognize them in the moment, but you will see them quickly enough. After them, you will never be the same again, for better or worse. A job promotion, a marriage, a divorce, a bankruptcy, an eviction, a sickness, or the death of a loved one: all can serve as defining moments in your life.

3. When faced with a defining moment, you control how it defines you.

If you do not get in front of your defining moment, you risk allowing the moment to define you in ways that are not positive or productive, leading to uncertainty and putting you at risk. You must be proactive, not reactive in such moments. You may not have produced the moment, but you do have the responsibility to manage it by responding positively and decisively so that it will shape you for the better.

Defining Moment for the Rich Young Ruler

> Just then a man came up to Jesus and asked, "Teacher, what good thing must I do to get eternal life?"
>
> "Why do you ask me about what is good?" Jesus replied. "There is only One who is good. If you want to enter life, keep the commandments."
>
> "Which ones?" he inquired.
>
> Jesus replied, "'You shall not murder, you shall not commit adultery, you shall not steal, you shall not give false testimony, honor your father and mother,' and 'love your neighbor as yourself.'"
>
> "All these I have kept," the young man said. "What do I still lack?"
>
> Jesus answered, "If you want to be perfect, go, sell your possessions and give to the poor, and you will have treasure in heaven. Then come, follow me."

> When the young man heard this, he went away sad, because he had great wealth. (Matthew 19:16-22, NIV)

We don't know much beyond the Bible account of this encounter between Jesus and the rich young ruler, but it is clear it was a defining moment for him. It is clear he was rich, young, and a ruler—a man of great influence and power. He had morals, and apparently believed in doing the right thing. He discloses that he obeyed many of the laws of that day. And clearly, he feels pretty good about himself. Feeling confident he was more than qualified for eternal life, he asks Jesus what else he needed to do. Jesus said, essentially, "Sell everything and come follow me." This was a defining moment for this young man—a once in a lifetime opportunity that does not come along very often (sometimes never again). He would get eternal life and get to hang out with Jesus if only he would sell everything he owned. For a businessman, this would be similar to getting the chance to work with Warren Buffett; to a computer expert, the chance to work with Bill Gates; to a technical genius, the chance to pick the mind of Steve Jobs; to a political aspirant, the chance to mingle with President Ronald Reagan; to the star wide receiver, the chance to play with football legend, Joe Namath; to the religious leader, the chance to be discipled by Mother Teresa. How could he possibly pass this up?

Unfortunately, the young man was unwilling to seize this grand destiny and settled for something less, allowing the opportunity of the defining moment to pass him by. The Bible says he went away very sad.

Position Yourself for a Beyond Ordinary Destiny

To be proactive in taking advantage of the opportunity of the defining moment, you must position yourself properly.

1. Keep priorities on target.

The rich young ruler had his priorities out of balance and this caused him to miss an incredible opportunity to follow Christ and receive eternal life. Make sure you're living a balanced life and your priorities are in line with your life values.

2. Keep your heart in the right place.

The rich young ruler's heart was set on money and power. Although he did many things right, you could tell that his heart was so filled with the love of power and money, it left little room for love for Jesus and others.

3. Refuse to listen to voices of compromise.

The voice of compromise is so loud, at times, it screams. The voice of faith is a still, small whisper of a voice. If you listen to it, compromise will convince you to sacrifice your integrity, morality, values, and conscience to find an average destiny. Only by following the voice of faith can you find your beyond ordinary destiny (#beyondordinarydestiny). The more you listen for and obey the voice of faith, the louder it will be in your life.

"The voice of compromise is so loud, at times, it screams. The voice of faith is a still, small whisper of a voice."

---

4. Keep your eyes on the potential before you.

The rich young ruler could not see the real potential for his life and could not conceive of a beyond ordinary destiny because he was blinded by power and money—he could not see beyond them. He could not see beyond himself. Those who would live beyond ordinary lives understand it is not all about them, and that their destiny is found as they love others and look beyond themselves. Our potential is as unlimited as the love we are able to show.

"Those who would live beyond ordinary lives understand it is not all about them, and that their destiny is found as they love others and look beyond themselves."

---

5. Keep your feet on the right path.

It doesn't take the mind of a rocket scientist to conclude that once your heart, ears, mind, and eyes are on the wrong things—or nothing more than yourself—you will stray from the beyond ordinary destiny you could have had. I'm sure the rich young ruler woke up one day a few weeks after this opportunity and said to himself, "Boy, did I mess this thing up badly." Deep down in his heart he must have realized he had missed out on the greatest opportunity of his life.

Life is a learning experience. Look back at your life over the past year . . . five years . . . ten years . . . and recall how you responded to defining moments in each of those periods. (Consider writing down these responses.) Then answer the following questions: How did you react? Why? What would you do differently now? Why? These are all very good learning points to help you better prepare for reacting even more positively to future defining moments, and insuring you will live out your beyond ordinary destiny.

Use your smartphone or tablet QR code reader to watch an important video about beyond ordinary living! Or, enter this link in your web browser: www.livingbeyondordinary.org/videos/chapter10.

Tweet these!

What does your destiny look like today, tomorrow, ten years from now? #beyondordinarydestiny http://bit.ly/1pVu3o1

What does a defining moment look like to you? #beyondordinarydefiningmoment http://bit.ly/1pVu3o1

"The greatest legacy one can pass on to one's children and grandchildren is not money or other material things accumulated in one's life, but rather a legacy of character and faith."—Billy Graham

~

"It is up to us to live up to the legacy that was left for us, and to leave a legacy that is worthy of our children and of future generations."
—Christine Gregoire

~

"When I look towards my future, I want to leave a legacy that runs rich."
—Kyle Shewfelt

~

"All good men and women must take responsibility to create legacies that will take the next generation to a level we could only imagine."—Jim Rohn

~

"Carve your name on hearts, not tombstones. A legacy is etched into the minds of others and the stories they share about you."—Shannon L. Alder

~

"What makes greatness is starting something that lives after you."
—Ralph Sockman

~

"To laugh often and much; to win the respect of intelligent people and the affection of children; to earn the appreciation of honest critics and endure the betrayal of false friends; to appreciate beauty, to find the best in others; to leave the world a bit better, whether by a healthy child, a garden patch or a redeemed social condition; to know even one life has breathed easier because you lived. This is to have succeeded."—Ralph Waldo Emerson

~

"Not well traveled, not well read, not well-to-do or well bred just want to hear instead, 'Well done, good and faithful one'"—Nichole Nordeman

~

"There is a defining moment in every person's life. Within that moment, everything that that person is shines its brightest."—Unknown

~

"Don't compromise yourself. You are all you've got."—Janis Joplin

~

CHAPTER 11

BEYOND ORDINARY LEGACY

What's the first impression that comes to mind when you hear each of the following names?

~ Billy Graham

~ Mother Teresa

~ Fidel Castro

~ Bill Clinton

~ Adolph Hitler

~ Nelson Mandela

~ Pope Benedict

~ Josef Stalin

~ Winston Churchill

~ John F. Kennedy

It can be argued that whatever came to your mind captured the legacy of each person above—at least in part. For example, for Mother Teresa, you might have thought, "ministry to the poorest of the poor," "love," or any number of other things. She left behind an incredible legacy of love that still inspires millions of people all over the world (#LivingBeyondOrdinary). Like her, each of these leaders has a legacy, defined as "something handed down from those who have gone before." However, as you can see from the list, it is possible to leave either a positive legacy or a negative one. Perhaps the best way to stay on track in living a beyond ordinary life is to keep ever before us the legacy we want to leave behind (#beyondordinarylegacy).

"Perhaps the best way to stay on track in living a beyond ordinary life is to keep ever before us the legacy we want to leave behind (#beyondordinarylegacy)."

A Legacy of Compassion and Hope

When we started the Community Food and Outreach Center, we did so purely from a collective heart to help people and bring them hope. As a Christian leader in our community, I've always had a heart of compassion to help people. I always root for the underdog, whether in football, basketball, soccer, or life in general—I always seem to pull for the person or team against which the cards seemed to be stacked. Although I had personally never really felt the depth of pain most of our clients and guests experience on a daily basis, by putting myself in their shoes, listening to their stories, and allowing myself to feel their pain, I gain some level of compassion and empathy. However, after walking through the death of the Destiny Foundation, I gained a deeper understanding of the pain, heartache, and despair of the people we serve. Now with a little more experience and conviction, I can look hurting people in the eye and say, "I've been there. I know what you are going through." Now I have a deeper understanding than ever before of the pain, and a much greater depth of compassion. I'm better for it and the people we help are better served because they know I'm speaking from experience.

A Legacy Beyond Our Expectations

It soon became obvious that it had been the right call to relaunch the mission. After months and months of hard work, we started to see the momentum build and the benefits of having a regional team work in our favor. Many people in the nonprofit world were shocked and very happy at the turnaround. For twelve years, we rented the 50,000 square foot building that had formerly been one of Orlando's first lumber yards, and made it a campus of hope.

In the summer of 2013, we applied for grants from the City of Orlando and Orange County to purchase the landmark building on 150 W. Michigan St. After months of filing, interviews, and applications, we had nothing left to do but wait for the big announcement of the grant award. Although we were confident, until we held the award letter in hand, nothing was final.

Within a few weeks of this, we received word from a large Christian ministry in our region I had worked with for many years. They were interested in helping us with the purchase as well. You've heard the old saying, "When it rains, it pours." Well, it was really pouring in for us. The ministry gave us a generous gift of $500,000, far exceeding any expectations we had.

Shortly thereafter, the week of the grant award announcement finally arrived. The City of Orlando and Orange County officially notified us that we would receive a $1 million grant, exceeding even our wildest dreams. John Maxwell says, "When momentum is against you, you can do nothing right; but, when momentum is for you, you can do nothing wrong." Needless to say, we were enjoying the positive momentum.

As all this great news was pouring in, I couldn't help but think of all the wonderful things that had happened over the years, and took time to dream that the legacy we established in Orlando would continue to bring help and hope to hundreds of thousands of families for the next 100 years. The dream is now stronger than ever. The future is bright as we continue to offer hope to the working poor in Central Florida.

Dream, Define, and Develop Your Legacy

Make sure yours is a lasting legacy, using what I call the "Three D's": Dream, Define, and Develop. Hundreds of times over the years, I have used this Three D principle as a leadership tool while leading everything from youth groups to nonprofits and churches.

A few years ago, I was leading a small group on a mission trip to Costa Rica. As in many cases when you go overseas, your American plans and goals are scrubbed once you land and realize you have to be flexible and flow with reality to accomplish the mission. (I have learned to never be so tied to my way of doing things that I cannot let go and adapt to a specific surrounding and circumstance.) On this trip, we were working with a local pastor of a congregation, and our plans and his plans weren't working at all. We were going nowhere—and fast. After a few days, I realized we had to do something to help salvage the trip. Unfortunately, the pastor seemed very comfortable with the status quo. He was very resistant to change and outside the box thinking, so it took me a few hours of politely challenging him before he finally accepted that we needed a change and a new mind-set. Then we walked through the Three D process.

Dreaming Stage

The first step to leaving a lasting legacy is to dream. When it's in this stage, you don't have all the "i's" dotted and "t's" crossed, but you have a dream or passion that drives you.

After reviewing the situation, we determined that our Sunday school approach for his community was not working. It was easy to make this assessment because no one was showing up for the summer camp. Looking around, it didn't take a genius to figure out that the people were hungry and consumed with wondering where they would get their next meal, so they were not nearly as concerned as we were about a religious summer camp program. We quickly determined that we needed to get food to the thousands of people in poverty in the community. Further, we needed to go to them, not make them come to us. The dream was to purchase 100 lb. bags of rice, go to the center of town, and simply start handing out smaller bags of rice to families in need.

When you're dreaming, think big. Think outside the box. Don't be limited by what's been done or what someone else is doing. Move beyond all that and let your imagination run wild.

Definition Stage

This is the stage where you begin to put some meat on the bones of your dream. You begin to narrow down the dream into more specific, practical steps. Although your dream is always a work in progress and it changes like any living organism, this is the step where you specifically articulate your dream so it can begin to take shape and form.

The reluctant pastor finally agreed to the initial plan, but wanted more than a dream; he wanted me to add some X's and O's to the idea of serving his community. Although I couldn't speak Spanish and he couldn't speak English, over lunch, I laid out the execution on a napkin and gave him some practical, easy steps he could wrap his head around. Aided by our interpreter, the lights came on and the pastor was quickly on board. As soon as I helped him define the dream, his comfort level and excitement level increased greatly.

Development Stage

The development stage is the hardest, and requires a lot of time and energy, but it is most satisfying and rewarding. This is the stage where you begin to put feet to the dream, take concrete action, and actually practice what you've been thinking about.

The time for execution was at hand. The rice was purchased, the plan was put in place, and it was time to put feet to the dream. Our team had been greatly disappointed because we had planned so diligently for a summer camp Sunday school, but in the new plan they caught a glimpse of hope, were filled with anticipation, and were ready to go.

In the development stage, as we shared the details, the pastor relapsed into the status quo, saying, "We have never done it this way before." If I heard him say this one time, I heard him say it 100 times. He said it so often, I memorized his words and could repeat the phrase to him in Spanish. (Not bad for someone who doesn't speak Spanish!) I didn't have the time or the heart to tell him that the eight words, "We have never done it this way before," were the favorite last words of dying organizations, and that he should try his best to avoid using the phrase because it is filled with doubt, unbelief, and defeat. I didn't have the heart to tell this pastor that I had never done what we planned either, but I was willing to take a risk.

Within several minutes of setting up our food distribution plan in the center of town, dozens of people came through the line not only for food, but for prayer and encouragement. Within an hour, hundreds of people were standing in line. Our team went back five or six times to purchase more rice from the town warehouse. This town had never seen anything like this in their town square. By that time, the pastor was beyond crying for joy; he was proud as a peacock, and filled with energy and enthusiasm. A dream with definition and development did all this for a small town in Costa Rica. It can work just as powerfully in your life.

Abraham's Beyond Ordinary Legacy

Abraham wanted a legacy, but in his time, these were passed down from father to son, and Abraham had no children. Worse yet, he and his wife, Sarah, were both well along in years—hopelessly beyond even the Viagra years. Deep down, they both knew they had little chance of ever having children of their own. That is, until God showed up.

The Lord's Beyond Ordinary Covenant with Abram (Abraham)

> After this, the word of the Lord came to Abram in a vision: "Do not be afraid, Abram. I am your shield, your very great reward."
>
> But Abram said, "Sovereign Lord, what can you give me since I remain childless and the one who will inherit my estate is Eliezer of Damascus?" And Abram said, "You have given me no children; so a servant in my household will be my heir."
>
> Then the word of the Lord came to him: "This man will not be your heir, but a son who is your own flesh and blood will be your heir." He took him outside and said, "Look up at the sky and count the stars—if indeed you can count them." Then he said to him, "So shall your offspring be."
>
> Abram believed the Lord, and he credited it to him as righteousness. (Genesis 15:1-6, NIV)

In this powerful story of legacy, we will see that Abraham, in the face of impossibility, had to demonstrate beyond ordinary courage, beyond ordinary vision, and beyond ordinary faith to build a beyond ordinary legacy.

Beyond Ordinary Courage

Notice the first thing God said to Abraham was not to fear. Fear can be the biggest obstacle we face when it comes to our legacy. When fear grips us, it can immobilize and paralyze us. Abraham needed beyond ordinary courage to even be in position to receive a beyond ordinary vision. To dare greatly and dream big, you must banish fear from your heart and mind.

Beyond Ordinary Vision

Although Abraham was in an impossible situation, he had the ability to see even the seemingly impossible becoming a reality. The second thing God asked him to do was to go outside his tent. We all have our "tents," boxes we live in that limit our vision and keep our dreams from becoming a reality. Inside our tent, we are unable to see the wide sky of possibility that allows us to dream big. Inside our tents, we become discouraged and filled with doubt, unable to see the limitless potential available to us. It is no wonder God called Abraham outside and told him to look up to the sky and count the stars. He wanted Abraham to feel the limitlessness he would need to receive the vision. He wanted Abraham to go beyond ordinary.

Many times, our situation changes when we simply step out of our limited surroundings and into the potential God has for us. Still, far too many of us remain in the small, comfortable tents of the status quo atmosphere, warm and cozy, leaving our legacy limited . . . average.

Beyond Ordinary Faith

I love how this part of Abraham's story ends. After this dramatic encounter in which God rocked Abraham's world with a renewed sense of legacy, verse 6 says, "Abram believed the Lord, and he credited it to him as righteousness" (Genesis 15:6, NIV). Abraham believed the Lord. That sounds so very simple, but many times it can be extremely difficult. Yet just such beyond ordinary faith is a key to receiving a big vision and creating a beyond ordinary legacy.

Jonathan Edwards' Beyond Ordinary Legacy

Husband and wife Jonathan and Sarah Edwards lived in colonial America in the early 1700s. They walked by faith, and consequently, left a legacy far beyond anything they could have imagined.

Jonathan Edwards felt God's call to become a minister, so he and his young bride accepted a pastorate over a small congregation. In the years that followed, he wrote many sermons, prayers, and books, and was influential in beginning the Great Awakening. Jonathan and Sarah produced eleven children who all grew to adulthood (unusual for the time). Sarah was a partner in her husband's ministry, and he sought her advice regarding sermons and church matters. They spent time talking about these things together, and when their children were old enough, the parents included them in the discussions.

The effect of the Edwards' lives has been far-reaching. The most telling results of their faithfulness to God's call are found in the lives of their descendants. In a research study in 1900, A.E. Winship lists a few of the accomplishments of the 1,400 Edwards descendants he was able to find:

100 lawyers and a dean of a law school

80 holders of public office

66 physicians and a dean of a medical school

65 professors of colleges and universities

30 judges

13 college presidents

3 mayors of large cities

3 governors of states

3 United States senators

1 comptroller of the United States Treasury

1 Vice President of the United States

Jonathan Edwards vs. Max Jukes
(A Case Study of the Legacies of Two Men)

A Brief Family History of Max Jukes: Max Jukes was an atheist who lived in New York during the nineteenth century.

Of Jukes' 560 known descendants:

7 were murderers

60 became thieves

67 reported having syphilis

100 were alcoholics

50% of the women in his family line became prostitutes

300 died prematurely

The Family History of Jonathan Edwards:

300 were preachers

295 were college graduates

100 were missionaries

100 were lawyers

80 held public office including 1 Vice President of the United States (Aaron Burr), 13 U.S. Senators, 1 state governor, 3 big city mayors and 1 U.S. comptroller

75 military officers

65 college professors including 13 college presidents

56 physicians including 1 Dean of Medical School[4]

We have a unique opportunity in life to establish a legacy that will inspire, enrich, and make a lasting impact on the generations that follow us. It is not all about us, it is about so much more.

"We have a unique opportunity in life to establish a legacy that will inspire, enrich, and make a lasting impact on the generations that follow us."

Numbers Don't Define Your Legacy

Americans draw a lot of comfort from numbers. We even tend to define ourselves by them. We like to keep score, see our standing in comparison to others, and more.

~ Our zip code defines where we live and how well off we must be.

~ Our salary determines our worth. The more money we make the more valuable and important we feel.

~ Our weight determines how easily we will be accepted.

~ Our bank account balance shows whether or not we have "arrived."

~ Our SAT score helps colleges determine our intelligence and likelihood of success.

As significant as they may sound and seem, we often overvalue numbers in defining our legacy. Legacies are about people and lives that are changed (#numbersdonotdefineme). I love what Shannon Alder says: "Carve your name on hearts, not tombstones. A legacy is etched into the minds of others and the stories they share about you."

Not long ago, a few friends from Edgewater High School called me and said they wanted to meet at our community center in downtown Orlando. One of them works very closely with the mayor of Orlando, so my first thought was that the purpose of the meeting was to plan an event at our campus in partnership with the City of Orlando. I didn't think much about it after the initial call.

When we finally met, I was just happy to see my old friends. We exchanged pleasantries and talked about the good old days for a bit. Then they handed me a formal letter that took me by surprise. The letter was from the Edgewater High School Foundation Board, informing me I had been chosen for induction into the Edgewater High School Hall of Fame. To say I was shocked would be an understatement.

I don't get many awards (I'm not really that important), so for me to get this recognition was unexpected. As soon as the shock wore off, I silently asked myself these questions: *I wonder if they know? What if they find out? What if they discover the truth? Will they take away the award?* Why the consternation? Well, I wasn't exactly a star student in high school. I like to say I was a very late bloomer, but the reality is, I just didn't apply myself—didn't try hard at all. I was more concerned with girls, surfing, and soccer than I was with academics. In fact, when final class "standings" came out in my senior year, I was number 748 in my class of around 920 students, safely within the bottom 20 percent of my graduating class. I wondered if I should tell them. (FYI, if any member of the board that selected me is reading this book right now, it's too late to take the honor away because the ceremony was held in April 2014!)

The more I thought about it, although I'm certainly not proud of my dismal class rank, I am proud to say I never let that 748 number define me—nor should you allow such numbers and other things in your past to define you. My legacy will be my passion for the past fifteen years: Offering a hand up to help people move beyond their circumstances and current situations, to find hope.

What kind of legacy do you want to leave when you are gone? What do you want people to say of you when they sum up your life in a sentence or two? What do you want to hand down to the generations that follow you? Last question (and it is a big one): What are you doing right now to ensure you leave this legacy?

Our legacy is bigger than our past and we continue to forge it every day. It's not too late for you to establish your beyond ordinary legacy. I believe you will.

Use your smartphone or tablet QR code reader to watch an important video about beyond ordinary living! Or, enter this link in your web browser: www.livingbeyondordinary.org/videos/chapter11.

Tweet these!

Who is your greatest hero and what is their legacy? #beyondordinarylegacy http://bit.ly/1pVu3o1

Which numbers have you allowed to define you—income? area code? #numbersdonotdefineme http://bit.ly/1pVu3o1

ABOUT THE AUTHOR

Nonprofit pioneer, speaker, and author, **Scott George**, has been a passionate and compassionate visionary and innovator in the church and nonprofit world for over thirty years. His unique ability to communicate leadership principles and insights have motivated and inspired groups of all sizes. He has traveled the world, bringing hope and help through philanthropic and humanitarian campaigns and outreaches. He currently serves as senior pastor of Pine Castle United Methodist Church in Orlando, Florida, and is the cofounder of Community Food and Outreach Center in downtown Orlando, an innovative, cutting edge nonprofit facility that serves thousands of families each month with food, medical care, crisis intervention, and education. Scott is happily married to Tammi, his wife, and has four beautiful children: Austen, Aaren, Amanda, and Allison .

J. Scott George
130 Galahad Lane
Maitland, FL 32751
Websites
www.livingbeyondordinary.org
www.communityfoodoutreach.org

Emails
jscottgeorge1@gmail.com
scott@communityfoodoutreach.org

Phone
(407) 579-8515

Social Media
Follow Scott George on Twitter: @RevJScottGeorge (https://twitter.com/RevJScottGeorge/)
Become a fan of Scott George on Facebook: J scott george (https://www.facebook.com/pages/J-scott-george/668980636525535)
Connect with Scott George on LinkedIn: J Scott George (https://www.linkedin.com/profile/view?id=237735739)
Watch Scott George on YouTube: J Scott (http://www.jscottgeorge.com/)

Speaking and Appearances
If you would like to schedule Scott George for a speaking engagement or appearance, please call, email, or write him, using the information above.

NOTES

1. Mother Teresa Quotes, Quotable Quotes, paraphrase of *The Paradoxical Commandments*, by Kent M. Keith, accessed July 7, 2014, http://www.goodreads.com/quotes/884217-people-are-often-unreasonable-and-self-centered-forgive-them-anyway-if, http://en.wikiquote.org/wiki/Mother_Teresa#Quotes.

2. Stephen Covey, *The 7 Habits of Highly Effective People, Habit 7: Sharpen the Saw*, accessed July 7, 2014, https://www.stephencovey.com/7habits/7habits-habit7.php.

3. "Vinko Bogataj," *Wikipedia*, last modified on 6 February 2014, http://en.wikipedia.org/wiki/Vinko_Bogataj.

4. A. E. Winship, "*Jukes-Edwards, A Study in Education and Heredity*," written 1900. *Posted: June 4th, 2012, website accessed July 2014,* https://www.unlockingthebible.org/jonathan-edwards-leaving-a-godly-legacy.

CPSIA information can be obtained at www.ICGtesting.com
Printed in the USA
LVOW12s1937021014

407004LV00004B/6/P